# A Closer Relationship With God

# A Closer Relationship With God

(Second Edition)

## Intimacy and Devotion

## Bill Vincent

Copyright © 2016 All rights reserved.

No part of this publication may be reproduced, stored in a retrieval system or transmitted in any way by any means, electronic, mechanical, photocopy, recording or otherwise, without the prior permission of the author except as provided by USA copyright law.

The opinions expressed by the author are not necessarily those of Revival Waves of Glory Books & Publishing.

Published by Revival Waves of Glory Books & Publishing
PO Box 596| Litchfield, Illinois 62056 USA
www.revivalwavesofgloryministries.com

Revival Waves of Glory Books & Publishing is committed to excellence in the publishing industry.

Book design copyright © 2016 by Revival Waves of Glory Books & Publishing. All rights reserved.

Paperback: 978-1-60796-966-2

Published in the United States of America

# Table of Contents

Chapter One Spiritual Maturity ............................................. 7
Chapter Two A Deeper Relationship ................................. 12
Chapter Three Important Decisions ................................... 17
Chapter Four A Love Relationship ..................................... 32
Chapter Five Make it Real .................................................. 35
Chapter Six The Fight of Faith ........................................... 39
Chapter Seven Daily Devotionals ....................................... 60
Chapter Eight Daily Bible Reading ................................... 104
About the Author .............................................................. 129
Recommended Books ....................................................... 131

# Introduction

This book is being released after months of seeing many with a need of a deeper intimacy with God. We all must learn to stay connected with God. After you read this book you are going to see for yourself what God says about it. Have you ever wondered if it's possible to have a meaningful relationship with God? This powerful study will help you discover for yourself how such a rewarding relationship with God is possible. The last two Chapters are Daily Bible Reading and Daily Devotions to help you to get on the right track in your walk with God. You will also learn how salvation is something you keep burning on the inside of you. You have to keep your fire burning and there are many things released in this book that will help you begin your journey to genuine faith.

# Chapter One
# Spiritual Maturity

We will begin this book by getting you to find your way in God through a spiritual maturity. As Christians grow in spiritual maturity, we hunger for an intimate relationship with Jesus, but at the same time we feel confused over how to go about it.

How do you get closer to the invisible God? How do you hold a conversation with someone who doesn't audibly talk back? This is the question that seems to be on all new Christian's lips.

Our confusion begins with the word "intimate," which has become cheapened because of our culture's obsession with sex. The essence of an intimate relationship, especially with Jesus, requires sharing. I want you to consider a relationship with God is similar to sharing your deepest thought with the one you love. It is much like a romance.

## Intimacy and Devotion

The Gospels are remarkable books. Even though they are not exhaustive biographies of Jesus of Nazareth, they give us a compelling portrait of him. If you read those four accounts carefully, you will come away knowing the secrets of his heart. The more you study Matthew, Mark, Luke, and John, the better you'll understand Jesus. When you meditate on his parables, you'll discover the love, compassion, and tenderness that flow from him. As you read about Jesus healing people thousands of years ago, you begin to grasp that our Living God can reach out from heaven and touch your life today. Through reading God's Word, your relationship with Jesus begins to take on new and deeper significance. Are you getting this? Spending time in God's Word will open up the sharing of God's heart to yours.

Jesus revealed his emotions. He got angry at injustice, showed concern about a hungry crowd of his followers, and cried when his friend Lazarus died. But the greatest thing is how you, personally, can make this knowledge of Jesus your own. He wants you to know him.

What sets the Bible apart from other books is that through it, God speaks to individuals. The Holy Spirit unfolds Scripture so it becomes a love letter written specifically to you. The more you desire relationship with Jesus, the more personal that letter becomes.

## Intimacy and Devotion

When you are intimate with someone else, you trust them enough to share your secrets. As God, already knows everything about you anyway, but when you choose to tell him what's hidden deep within you, it proves you trust him. This is sharing.

Trust is hard. You've probably been betrayed by other people, and when that happened, maybe you swore you'd never open up again. But Jesus loved you and trusted you first. He laid down his life for you. That sacrifice has earned him your trust.

Many of my secrets are sad, and maybe yours are too. It hurts to bring them up again and give them to Jesus, but that is the path to intimacy. If you want the closest of relationships with Jesus, you have to risk opening your heart. There's no other way. As you open your heart up to God by sharing you will feel His love through the friendship with Him.

When you share yourself in relationship with Jesus, when you talk to him often and step out in faith, he will reward you by giving you more of himself. Stepping out takes courage, and it takes time. Held back by our fears, we can move beyond them only through the encouragement of the Holy Spirit.

At first you may notice no difference in your connection with Jesus, but over weeks and months, Bible verses will take on new meaning for you. The bond will grow stronger. In small doses, life will make more sense. Gradually you will sense that Jesus is there, listening to your prayers, answering through Scripture and promptings in your heart. There will be a sureness that will come upon you that something wonderful is happening.

Jesus never turns away anyone who seeks him. He will give you every help you need to build an intense, intimate relationship with him.

When two people are intimate, they don't need words. Husbands and wives, as well as best friends, know the pleasure of simply being together. They can enjoy each other's company, even in silence. A husband will know things his wife is thinking just by a certain look.

We glorify God by loving and serving him, and we can do that better when we have an intimate relationship with Jesus Christ, his Son. As an adopted member of this family, you possess the right to enjoy your Father God and your Savior as well.

## Intimacy and Devotion

You were meant for intimacy with Jesus. It is your most important calling now, and for eternity. God will truly change your life through His son Jesus Christ.

# Chapter Two
## A Deeper Relationship

I know it may seem difficult to get to know God in a deeper way. I have to tell you God is calling you to a deeper relationship today. With the Holy Spirit directing your life, you will experience a deeper relationship with God and you will grow in your ability to trust Him.

What does it mean to grow in your relationship with Jesus? Growing in your relationship with Jesus means to know Him better, to love and obey Him more. This also means living your life and with the help of the Holy Spirit you can be like Jesus.

John 17:3 And this is life eternal, that they might know thee the only true God, and Jesus Christ, whom thou hast sent.

## Intimacy and Devotion

Matthew 22:37, 38 Jesus said unto him, Thou shalt love the Lord thy God with all thy heart, and with all thy soul, and with all thy mind. This is the first and great commandment.

Your growing love for God will lead you to obey His commandments.

John 14:21 He that hath my commandments, and keepeth them, he it is that loveth me: and he that loveth me shall be loved of my Father, and I will love him, and will manifest myself to him.

Just as it's natural for a child to grow in a loving relationship with a parent, it is also natural for you to grow in your love relationship with God.

How can you grow in your relationship with Jesus?

Communication is vital to any relationship. Several aspects of communication will help you develop your relationship with Jesus.

- God communicates with us through the Bible, revealing His character and His will.

- 2 Timothy 3:16, 17 All scripture *is* given by inspiration of God, and *is* profitable for doctrine, for reproof, for correction, for instruction in righteousness: That the man of God may be perfect, throughly furnished unto all good works.
- We communicate with God through prayer, sharing our thoughts, our needs and our desire to do his will.

Philippians 4:6, 7 Be careful for nothing; but in every thing by prayer and supplication with thanksgiving let your requests be made known unto God. And the peace of God, which passeth all understanding, shall keep your hearts and minds through Christ Jesus.

1 John 5:14, 15 And this is the confidence that we have in him, that, if we ask any thing according to his will, he heareth us: And if we know that he hear us, whatsoever we ask, we know that we have the petitions that we desired of him.

These verses tell us we can pray about everything. When we pray according to God's will, he hears us and answers us. Thanking God is also part of praying.

1 Thessalonians 5:18 In every thing give thanks: for this is the will of God in Christ Jesus concerning you.

Ephesians 5:20 Giving thanks always for all things unto God and the Father in the name of our Lord Jesus Christ;

- We communicate with Christians through fellowship, encouraging and building up one another.
- Hebrews 10:24, 25 And let us consider one another to provoke unto love and to good works: Not forsaking the assembling of ourselves together, as the manner of some *is;* but exhorting *one another:* and so much the more, as ye see the day approaching.

It is important to spend time with other Christians to encourage each other to love and do good. I'm talking about those who live a life for God more than just on Sundays. We need to share our Christian experience with others who love God, and likewise allow them to share with us. God appoints the church as a place for us to meet other Christians and learn about God.

- We communicate with others who don't know God personally by sharing about our relationship with Jesus.

Acts 4:12 Neither is there salvation in any other: for there is none other name under heaven given among men, whereby we must be saved.

Set aside a time and place for daily personal Bible study and prayer. A good book to begin with is the New Testament Book of John. As you read, underline verses you find particularly meaningful. Pray and ask God to show you who He is and how you can respond to Him.

As you rely on the Holy Spirit for power, read the Bible, pray, spend time with other believers and tell people about Jesus, God will produce His character in you and you will mature spiritually.

- Keys to spiritual growth:
- Understanding your relationship with Jesus
- Experiencing God's love and forgiveness
- Power for living a dynamic Christian life

# Chapter Three
# Important Decisions

When you become a Christian, from the very start you will find yourself with many important decisions. A personal relationship with Jesus is the most important decision you could ever make in your life. It is unlike any other relationship. Jesus will be with you every step of the way. When you step out of this life and into eternity if you do not have this relationship, you will spend eternity apart from Him.

So, if you will allow us, we'd like to tell you how you can come into a personal relationship with Jesus.

God desires a personal relationship with you. God created you. And He didn't just create you to exist all alone and apart from Him. He created you with a view to coming into a personal relationship with Him.

## Intimacy and Devotion

Genesis 1:27 So God created man in his *own* image, in the image of God created he him; male and female created he them.

Remember, God had face-to-face encounters and fellowship with Adam and Eve, the first couple. And just as God fellowshipped with them, so He desires to fellowship with you.

Genesis 3:18, 19 Thorns also and thistles shall it bring forth to thee; and thou shalt eat the herb of the field; In the sweat of thy face shalt thou eat bread, till thou return unto the ground; for out of it wast thou taken: for dust thou *art*, and unto dust shalt thou return.

1 John 1:5-7 This then is the message which we have heard of him, and declare unto you, that God is light, and in him is no darkness at all. If we say that we have fellowship with him, and walk in darkness, we lie, and do not the truth: But if we walk in the light, as he is in the light, we have fellowship one with another, and the blood of Jesus Christ his Son cleanseth us from all sin.

John 3:16 For God so loved the world, that he gave his only begotten Son, that whosoever believeth in him should not perish, but have everlasting life.

## Intimacy and Devotion

God love you and you need to always remember that. Humanity has a sin problem that blocks a relationship with god. When Adam and Eve chose to sin against God in the Garden of Eden, they catapulted the entire human race which they gave birth into sin. Since the time of Adam and Eve, every human being has been born into the world with a propensity to sin.

The apostle Paul confirmed that sin entered the world through one man, and death through sin.

Romans 5:12 Wherefore, as by one man sin entered into the world, and death by sin; and so death passed upon all men, for that all have sinned:

Indeed, we are told that through the disobedience of the one man many were made sinners.

Romans 5:19 For as by one man's disobedience many were made sinners, so by the obedience of one shall many be made righteous.

1 Corinthians 15:21, 22 For since by man *came* death, by man *came* also the resurrection of the dead. For as in Adam all die, even so in Christ shall all be made alive.

## Intimacy and Devotion

Jesus often spoke of sin in metaphors that illustrate the mess of sin can wreak in one's life. He described sin as blindness, sickness, being enslaved in bondage, and living in darkness. Moreover, Jesus taught that this is a universal condition and that all people are guilty before God.

**Matthew 23:16-26** Woe unto you, *ye* blind guides, which say, Whosoever shall swear by the temple, it is nothing; but whosoever shall swear by the gold of the temple, he is a debtor! *Ye* fools and blind: for whether is greater, the gold, or the temple that sanctifieth the gold? And, Whosoever shall swear by the altar, it is nothing; but whosoever sweareth by the gift that is upon it, he is guilty. *Ye* fools and blind: for whether *is* greater, the gift, or the altar that sanctifieth the gift? Whoso therefore shall swear by the altar, sweareth by it, and by all things thereon. And whoso shall swear by the temple, sweareth by it, and by him that dwelleth therein. And he that shall swear by heaven, sweareth by the throne of God, and by him that sitteth thereon. Woe unto you, scribes and Pharisees, hypocrites! for ye pay tithe of mint and anise and cummin, and have omitted the weightier *matters* of the law, judgment, mercy, and faith: these ought ye to have done, and not to leave the other undone. *Ye* blind guides, which strain at a gnat, and swallow a camel. Woe unto you, scribes and Pharisees, hypocrites! for ye make clean the outside of the cup and of the platter, but within they are full of extortion and excess. *Thou* blind Pharisee, cleanse first that *which is* within the cup and platter, that the outside of them may be clean also.

Matthew 9:12 But when Jesus heard *that,* he said unto them, They that be whole need not a physician, but they that are sick.

John 8:34 Jesus answered them, Verily, verily, I say unto you, Whosoever committeth sin is the servant of sin.

John 8:12 Then spake Jesus again unto them, saying, I am the light of the world: he that followeth me shall not walk in darkness, but shall have the light of life.

John 12:35-46 Then Jesus said unto them, Yet a little while is the light with you. Walk while ye have the light, lest darkness come upon you: for he that walketh in darkness knoweth not whither he goeth. While ye have light, believe in the light, that ye may be the children of light. These things spake Jesus, and departed, and did hide himself from them. But though he had done so many miracles before them, yet they believed not on him: That the saying of Esaias the prophet might be fulfilled, which he spake, Lord, who hath believed our report? and to whom hath the arm of the Lord been revealed? Therefore they could not believe, because that Esaias said again, He hath blinded their eyes, and hardened their heart; that they should not see with *their* eyes, nor understand with *their* heart, and be converted, and I should heal them. These things said Esaias, when he saw his glory, and spake of him. Nevertheless among the chief rulers also many believed on him; but because of the Pharisees they did not confess *him,* lest they should be put out of the synagogue: For they loved the praise of men more than the praise of God. Jesus cried and said, He that believeth on me, believeth not on me, but on him that sent me. And he that seeth me seeth him that sent me. I am come a light into the world, that whosoever believeth on me should not abide in darkness.

Luke 7:37, 38 And, behold, a woman in the city, which was a sinner, when she knew that *Jesus* sat at meat in the Pharisee's house, brought an alabaster box of ointment, And stood at his feet behind *him* weeping, and began to wash his feet with tears, and did wipe *them* with the hairs of her head, and kissed his feet, and anointed *them* with the ointment.

Jesus also taught that both inner thoughts and external acts render a person guilty. He taught that from within the human heart come evil thoughts, sexual immorality, theft, murder, adultery, greed, malice, deceit, envy, slander, arrogance, and folly. Moreover, He affirmed that God is fully aware of every person's sins, both external acts and inner thoughts; nothing escapes His notice.

Mark 5:28 For she said, If I may touch but his clothes, I

shall be whole.

Mark 7:21-23 For from within, out of the heart of men, proceed evil thoughts, adulteries, fornications, murders, Thefts, covetousness, wickedness, deceit, lasciviousness, an evil eye, blasphemy, pride, foolishness: All these evil things come from within, and defile the man.

Matthew 22:18 But Jesus perceived their wickedness, and said, Why tempt ye me, *ye* hypocrites?

Luke 6:8 But he knew their thoughts, and said to the man which had the withered hand, Rise up, and stand forth in the midst. And he arose and stood forth.

John 4:17-19 The woman answered and said, I have no husband. Jesus said unto her, Thou hast well said, I have no husband: For thou hast had five husbands; and he whom thou now hast is not thy husband: in that saidst thou truly. The woman saith unto him, Sir, I perceive that thou art a prophet.

Some people are more morally upright than others. But we all fall short of God's infinite standards. All human beings ultimately fall short of the task. Similarly, all of us fall short of measuring up to God's perfect holy standards.

Romans 3:23 For all have sinned, and come short of the glory of God;

Though the sin problem is a serious one, God has graciously provided a solution. Jesus died for our sins and made salvation possible. God's absolute holiness demands that sin be punished. The good news of the gospel, however, is that Jesus has taken this punishment on Himself. God loves us so much that He sent Jesus to bear the penalty for our sins!

Jesus confirmed that it was for the very purpose of dying that He came into the world. He perceived His death as being a sacrificial offering for the sins of humanity. Jesus took His sacrificial mission with utmost seriousness, for He knew that without Him, humanity would certainly perish and spend eternity apart from God in a place of great suffering.

John 12:27 Now is my soul troubled; and what shall I say? Father, save me from this hour: but for this cause came I unto this hour.

Matthew 26:26-28 And as they were eating, Jesus took bread, and blessed *it,* and brake *it,* and gave *it* to the disciples, and said, Take, eat; this is my body. And he took the cup, and gave thanks, and gave *it* to them, saying, Drink ye all of it; For this is my blood of the new testament, which is shed for many for the remission of sins.

Matthew 16:25 For whosoever will save his life shall lose it: and whosoever will lose his life for my sake shall find it.

Matthew 10:28 And fear not them which kill the body, but are not able to kill the soul: but rather fear him which is able to destroy both soul and body in hell.

Matthew 11:23 And thou, Capernaum, which art exalted unto heaven, shalt be brought down to hell: for if the mighty works, which have been done in thee, had been done in Sodom, it would have remained until this day.

Matthew 23:33 *Ye* serpents, *ye* generation of vipers, how can ye escape the damnation of hell?

Matthew 25:41 Then shall he say also unto them on the left hand, Depart from me, ye cursed, into everlasting fire, prepared for the devil and his angels:

Luke 16:22-28 And it came to pass, that the beggar died, and was carried by the angels into Abraham's bosom: the rich man also died, and was buried; And in hell he lift up his eyes, being in torments, and seeth Abraham afar off, and Lazarus in his bosom. And he cried and said, Father Abraham, have mercy on me, and send Lazarus, that he may dip the tip of his finger in water, and cool my tongue; for I am tormented in this flame. But Abraham said, Son, remember that thou in thy lifetime receivedst thy good things, and likewise Lazarus evil things: but now he is comforted, and thou art tormented. And beside all this, between us and you there is a great gulf fixed: so that they which would pass from hence to you cannot; neither can they pass to us, that *would come* from thence. Then he said, I pray thee therefore, father, that thou wouldest send him to my father's house: For I have five brethren; that he may testify unto them, lest they also come into this place of torment.

Jesus therefore described His mission this way: The Son of Man did not come to be served, but to serve, and to give his life as a ransom for many. The Son of Man came to seek and to save what was lost, for God did not send his Son into the world to condemn the world, but to save the world through him.

Matthew 20:28 Even as the Son of man came not to be ministered unto, but to minister, and to give his life a ransom for many.

Luke 19:10 For the Son of man is come to seek and to save that which was lost.

John 3:17 For God sent not his Son into the world to condemn the world; but that the world through him might be saved.

But the benefits of Christ's death on the cross are not automatically applied to your life. God requires you to believe in Jesus Christ.

By His sacrificial death on the cross, Jesus took the sins of the entire world on Himself and made salvation available for everyone. But this salvation is not automatic. Only those who personally choose to believe in Christ are saved.

1 John 2:2 And he is the propitiation for our sins: and not for ours only, but also for *the sins of* the whole world.

This is the consistent testimony of the biblical Jesus. Listen to His words:

John 3:16 For God so loved the world, that he gave his only begotten Son, that whosoever believeth in him should not perish, but have everlasting life.

John 6:40 And this is the will of him that sent me, that every one which seeth the Son, and believeth on him, may have everlasting life: and I will raise him up at the last day.

John 11:25 Jesus said unto her, I am the resurrection, and the life: he that believeth in me, though he were dead, yet shall he live:

Choosing not to believe in Jesus, by contrast, leads to eternal condemnation:

John 3:18 He that believeth on him is not condemned: but he that believeth not is condemned already, because he hath not believed in the name of the only begotten Son of God.

When you believe in Christ the Savior, a wonderful thing happens. God forgives you of all your sins. All of them! He puts them completely out of His sight. Ponder for a few minutes the

Intimacy and Devotion

following verses, which speak of the forgiveness of those who have believed in Christ:

Ephesians 1:7 In whom we have redemption through his blood, the forgiveness of sins, according to the riches of his grace;

Hebrews 10:17, 18 And their sins and iniquities will I remember no more. Now where remission of these *is, there is* no more offering for sin.

Psalms 32:1, 2 *A Psalm* of David, Maschil. Blessed *is he whose* transgression *is* forgiven, *whose* sin *is* covered. Blessed *is* the man unto whom the LORD imputeth not iniquity, and in whose spirit *there is* no guile.

Psalms 103:11, 12 For as the heaven is high above the earth, *so* great is his mercy toward them that fear him. As far as the east is from the west, *so* far hath he removed our transgressions from us.

Such forgiveness is wonderful indeed, for none of us can possibly work our way into heaven, or be good enough to warrant God's good favor. Because of what Jesus has done for us, we freely receive the gift of salvation. It is a gift provided solely through the grace of God. And all of it is ours by simply believing in Jesus.

Ephesians 2:8, 9 For by grace are ye saved through faith; and that not of yourselves: *it is* the gift of God: Not of works, lest any man should boast.

It is a highly dangerous thing to put off turning to Christ for salvation, for you do not know the day of your death. What if it happens this evening?

Ecclesiastics 7:2 *It is* better to go to the house of mourning, than to go to the house of feasting: for that *is* the end of all men; and the living will lay *it* to his heart.

If God is speaking to your heart now, then now is your door of opportunity to believe. God says in His Word that if you confess your sins He is faithful and just to forgive you.

Isaiah 55:6 Seek ye the LORD while he may be found, call ye upon him while he is near:

## Intimacy and Devotion

It starts with a Prayer. Would you like to place your faith in Jesus for the forgiveness of sins, thereby guaranteeing your eternal place in heaven along His side? If so, pray the following prayer with me.Keep in mind that it's not the prayer itself that saves you. It is the faith in your heart that saves you. So, let the following prayer be a simple expression of the faith that is in your heart:

Dear Jesus, I believe you are the Son of God. I believe that you died for me and arose on the third day. I ask you to forgive me of all my sins unto salvation. I thank you God is Jesus Name Amen.

Welcome to God's forever family. On the authority of the Word of God, we can now assure you that you are a part of God's forever family. If you prayed the above prayer with a heart of faith, you will spend all eternity by the side of Jesus in heaven. Welcome to God's family! Remember if you do sin remember it separates you from God and you will need to repent or turn away from your sin. Don't miss the very important Chapter Fight of Faith.

# Chapter Four
## A Love Relationship

Your relationship with God should be that of love. Love is the center of why God sent His son in the first place.

You know how passionate a deep love relationship between a man and a woman can be? They would do ANYTHING for each other... they would even DIE for each other... their love is so strong that NOTHING can keep them apart! That kind of a love relationship doesn't begin to describe how deep and powerful and passionate our love relationship with God is supposed to be!

Did you know that even BEFORE we were reconciled with our heavenly Father, He loved us so much that even death didn't stand in the way of Him trying to reconcile with us? That's right! We aren't loved for what we've done, but for who we are!

# Intimacy and Devotion

Romans 5:8 But God commendeth his love toward us, in that, while we were yet sinners, Christ died for us.

I have a challenge for you today... go turn on some powerful and passionate love songs, and then sing along, and instead of thinking about another person, think about your love relationship with your heavenly Father... think of His love relationship with you! For example, turn on the Un-chained Melody, an old classic passionate love song, and picture it as if your heavenly Father is singing it to you. When you do... be sure to listen to the words and let them sink in as you're singing along!

I am warning you... have a big box of tissues handy... you'll need them!! Any time you don't know what to do in pressing into God play worship music.

In Ephesians 3:17-19 clearly shows us that in order to experience the fullness of God in our lives, we MUST come to know how deep and passionate His love for us really is!

Ephesians 3:17-19 That Christ may dwell in your hearts by faith; that ye, being rooted and grounded in love, May be able to comprehend with all saints what *is* the breadth, and length, and depth, and height; And to know the love of Christ, which passeth knowledge, that ye might be filled with all the fulness of God.

## Intimacy and Devotion

I'm not trying to say that we are to have a romantic or sensual relationship with God, as in only unique to a relationship between a man and a woman, but what I am saying is that God wants a very lively, passionate, and intimate love relationship with us each day of our lives! If husband and wife can love each other so much that their love serves as a driving force that would cause either of them to give their lives for one another... shouldn't our relationship with God exceed that? Should not our relationship with God be greater than any earthly relationship we could ever have? Jesus wanted to have this kind of a relationship so much with you that He gave His life for it!

# Chapter Five
## Make it Real

We must make our relationship with God as real as possible not religious. Have you ever wondered if it's possible to have a meaningful relationship with God? An authentic relationship that works in the day-in-and-day-out circumstances of life? Do you hunger for a genuine experience of community and of God?

This is a study that will help you discover for yourself how such a relationship is possible. The Bible is the source to see what God has to say about the relationship He wants to have with you and about the community He wants to bring you into.

I have some questions concerning Churches all over the world. How do they feel about life? ....about God? Do they have a religion that works? ....a belief, a relationship that has changed their lives? One that they feel is authentic?

Have you ever wondered what we have to do, what we have to become in order to merit a relationship with God?

Romans 5:6, 7 For when we were yet without strength, in due time Christ died for the ungodly. For scarcely for a righteous man will one die: yet peradventure for a good man some would even dare to die.

God demonstrates His own love toward us, in that while we were yet sinners, Christ died for us. Much more then, having now been justified by His blood, we shall be saved from the wrath of God through Him. If while we were enemies we were reconciled to God through the death of His Son, much more, having been reconciled, we shall be saved by His life. And not only this, but we also triumph in God through our Lord Jesus Christ, through whom we have now received the reconciliation.

Sinners means: people who basically run their own lives, doing things their own way rather than God's way. Therefore they fall short of God's standard and separate themselves from God.

Justified means: to be acquitted, to be declared not guilty, to be made righteous, to be put in right standing.

Reconciled means: to no longer be at enmity (or enemies) with one another. The dictionary definition is "to make friends again; to win over; to settle a quarrel, a disagreement; to make satisfied; to be no longer opposed." To change from being at enmity (or separated) to becoming friends.

We didn't become sinners at enmity with God because God pulled away from mankind, abandoning us, leaving us on our own. Our relationship with God was damaged by man's own willfulness. At the beginning of creation, Adam and Eve, the first man and woman God created, made a choice to listen to someone else rather than to God. Like rebellious children, they walked away from the protection of being obedient to their Creator and Sustainer. Adam's decision to eat something God had for-bidden him to eat broke his intimacy with God. Consequently we became ungodly sinners, enemies of God.

Jesus didn't stay dead. He rose from the dead. He lives and we will live too, saved by His life.

The question you need to ask yourself is this: Where do you stand in your relationship with God if the Bible is true? Are you a sinner, ungodly, and an enemy of God? According to what you have read, is there hope for you? Can you have an authentic relationship with God?

## Intimacy and Devotion

Have you received reconciliation and become God's friend or does there seem to be something standing in your way? If it's the latter, do not despair. There is hope. Simply talk to God about it. Tell Him where you think you are and what your questions are. Then wait for Him to answer. He will, because He longs to have an intimate and meaningful relationship with you!

# Chapter Six
## The Fight of Faith

**DISOBEDIENCE IS CONTAGIOUS.**

HAVE YOU EVER seen a person start their walk on fire for Jesus, only to end up in a lukewarm state after a process of time? You wonder, how could someone so enthusiastic end up so weary in their walk? These people are the casualties of a battle they failed to recognize. Jude wrote a letter devoted entirely to addressing this conflict.

Jude 1:3 Beloved, when I gave all diligence to write unto you of the common salvation, it was needful for me to write unto you, and exhort you that ye should earnestly contend for the faith which was once delivered unto the saints.

Can you sense the urgency of the message? It is one of great importance.

To contend is to battle or combat. The word earnestly indicates serious intent. We must ask this question, with what or with whom do we fight? I have heard different answers to this question. One suggests that we battle for the faith by speaking of our resistance toward demons in the Heavenlies.

This is a valid answer of spiritual warfare.

Ephesians 6:10-12 Finally, my brethren, be strong in the Lord, and in the power of his might. Put on the whole armour of God, that ye may be able to stand against the wiles of the devil. For we wrestle not against flesh and blood, but against principalities, against powers, against the rulers of the darkness of this world, against spiritual wickedness in high *places.*

It is not the fight of which Jude is speaking. We can find the answer in the next statement in his letter.

Jude 1:4 For there are certain men crept in unawares, who were before of old ordained to this condemnation, ungodly men, turning the grace of our God into lasciviousness, and denying the only Lord God, and our Lord Jesus Christ.

We must battle for the faith because certain individuals have slipped into our churches misrepresenting the grace of God as a cover-up or even license for sin. The Greek word for lewdness is aselgeia. Strong's dictionary of Greek New Testament words defines this as "lasciviousness, unbridled lust or excess." These individuals pervert the grace of God by living excessive, fleshly lifestyles while proclaiming their salvation by grace. The Living Bible sheds further light on this. It declares these people show that after we become Christians we can do just as we like without fear of God's punishment. Jude said these men also "deny the only Lord God and our Lord Jesus Christ"

Some of you may be thinking, No one could come into our churches today and speak out a denial of God and our Lord Jesus Christ. You're right anyone who tried to do that couldn't get away with it anymore today than they could in Jude's day. But Jude indicated these people creep in unnoticed. No one who openly denies Jesus as the Christ could remain unnoticed. The following verse sheds some light on how these people manage to creep in:

Titus 1:15-16 Unto the pure all things are pure: but unto them that are defiled and unbelieving is nothing pure; but even their mind and conscience is defiled. They profess that they know God; but in works they deny him, being abominable, and disobedient, and unto every good work reprobate.

They do not deny the Lord by what they say but do so by their lifestyles or actions. At the same time they believe they know the Lord! Paul called such people impostors.

2 Timothy 3:13 But evil men and seducers shall wax worse and worse, deceiving, and being deceived.

An impostor is one who deceives others by an assumed character or false pretense (like the wolf in sheep's clothing). Paul did not limit their deception to others he said their influence extended to their own selves. They really believe they serve the Lord. They confess a new birth experience, speaking fluently in the language of the Scriptures as they participate in Christian activities. The only way to discern them is by the fruit of their lives.

Matthew 7:18-20 A good tree cannot bring forth evil fruit, neither *can* a corrupt tree bring forth good fruit. Every tree that bringeth not forth good fruit is hewn down, and cast into the fire. Wherefore by their fruits ye shall know them.

These imposters defile the flesh, reject authority, and speak evil of dignitaries. They are grumblers, complainers, walking according to their own lusts, desires; and they mouth great swelling words, flattering people to gain advantage. These are sensual worldly minded persons, who cause divisions. Is this not an accurate description of many who create problems in homes, ministries, and churches? Many naive, innocent people have been influenced by their behavior.

Jude 1:11 Woe unto them! for they have gone in the way of Cain, and ran greedily after the error of Balaam for reward, and perished in the gainsaying of Core.

He compares these people with three men of the Old Testament Cain, Balaam, and Korah, all who at one time enjoyed fellowship with God or was in the service of God. Cain presented a disobedient offering, became offended, rebelled against the counsel of God, and committed a murder. Balaam was greedy for power, position money and he prostituted the anointing on his life. Because of this, Balaam died by the edge of the sword at God's command.

Joshua 13:22 Balaam also the son of Beor, the soothsayer, did the children of Israel slay with the sword among them that were slain by them.

Korah was a priest and a descendant of Levi, yet he rose up in opposition to Moses and Aaron in the wilderness, claiming, You take too much upon yourselves. Why then do you exalt yourselves above the assembly of the Lord?

Numbers 16:3 And they gathered themselves together against Moses and against Aaron, and said unto them, *Ye take* too much upon you, seeing all the congregation *are* holy, every one of them, and the LORD *is* among them: wherefore then lift ye up yourselves above the congregation of the LORD?

His concern was not that Moses was overburdened; he wanted a share of Moses' authority. His hidden agenda was to promote himself. Insubordinate to God's appointed leadership; he accused Moses (whom God had exalted) of exalting himself. By doing this, Korah set himself against God's authority. His rebellion was judged when he was swallowed alive by the earth.

Romans 13:1, 2 Let every soul be subject unto the higher powers. For there is no power but of God: the powers that be are ordained of God. Whosoever therefore resisteth the power, resisteth the ordinance of God: and they that resist shall receive to themselves damnation.

## Intimacy and Devotion

Numbers 16:31-33 And it came to pass, as he had made an end of speaking all these words, that the ground clave asunder that *was* under them: And the earth opened her mouth, and swallowed them up, and their houses, and all the men that *appertained* unto Korah, and all *their* goods. They, and all that *appertained* to them, went down alive into the pit, and the earth closed upon them: and they perished from among the congregation.

Cain, Balaam, and Korah were unable to maintain their relationships with God because their goal was to serve themselves. It was not the service of God or His people they sought. Jude described these people further by saying:

Jude 1:12 These are spots in your feasts of charity, when they feast with you, feeding themselves without fear: clouds they are without water, carried about of winds; trees whose fruit withereth, without fruit, twice dead, plucked up by the roots;

Love feasts were common meals eaten together by the early church. Any sort of Christian gathering today could represent a love feast. The imposters who attended these feasts were called "spots" because of their conduct. Jesus is coming back for a "glorious church, not having spot of wrinkle or any such thing". Imposters will not be found in the assembly of the righteous on the Day of the Lord. Jude continues:

They are clouds without water, carried about by the winds.

## JUDE 12

Ephesians 5:27 That he might present it to himself a glorious church, not having spot, or wrinkle, or any such thing; but that it should be holy and without blemish.

Clouds without water illustrate the emptiness of their condition. Though they bear a semblance of godliness, they are void of the character of Jesus. They have the appearance of a believer without the life or substance of one. Take a careful look at the next statement made concerning these people.

Late autumn trees without fruit, twice dead, pulled up by the roots. JUDE 12

Jude compares them to late autumn trees with no fruit. Autumn is the time of harvest when fruit should be fully ripe and hanging on the tree. He described these barren, uprooted trees as "twice dead." What a description twice dead! In order to be twice dead you would have to be once dead, be made alive, and then die again. This describes people who were dead without Christ, then received salvation only to die again because they permanently departed from Him in their hearts.

## ONCE SAVED ALWAYS SAVED?

A very deceptive doctrine has been propagated throughout the church. It claims that once an individual is saved there is no way they can ever lose their salvation.

It is a controversial subject, yet it need not be. The only reason it is controversial is because some teachings have twisted the Scriptures until they say what we want to hear as opposed to God's truth. If a person's heart is set on an issue, they will funnel all Scripture through what they believe rather than believe what they read.

I challenge you to examine what the Bible has to say about it. Don't filter these scriptures through the teaching of Dr. So-and-So, but compare verse to verse and hear what the Spirit of God is saying.

Listen with your heart; it will not lie to you. There is no reason to fear truth if you love God. For if you truly love Him, you will never want to leave Him!

We first need to determine which verses refer to individuals who have been saved. There is a good example in James.

James 5:19, 20 Brethren, if any of you do err from the truth, and one convert him; Let him know, that he which converteth the sinner from the error of his way shall save a soul from death, and shall hide a multitude of sins.

Notice James said "brethren" and "if anyone among you." He was not addressing those who just think they are Christians; he was describing a believer who had wandered from the way of truth. Again note that James called a brother who wandered from the truth a sinner. If they are not turned back by repentance, their destination is death. Jude described them as "twice dead." It is obvious from James these people were once alive in Jesus. The Book of Proverbs amplifies this point.

Proverbs 21:16 The man that wandereth out of the way of understanding shall remain in the congregation of the dead.

In order to wander from the truth you must first walk in it. But once a person wanders from the truth, if he or she does not return to the path of righteousness, their final destination will be "the assembly of the dead," which is hell. Peter wrote:

2 Peter 2:20 For if after they have escaped the pollutions of the world through the knowledge of the Lord and Saviour Jesus Christ, they are again entangled therein, and overcome, the latter end is worse with them than the beginning.

Before we go on, ask yourself, would a person who has escaped the pollution of this world by the knowledge of the Lord Jesus Christ be saved? Without a doubt you should answer yes. So Peter is talking about people who have been saved. Now let's continue:

2 Peter 2:20b-21 they are again entangled therein, and overcome, the latter end is worse with them than the beginning. For it had been better for them not to have known the way of righteousness, than, after they have known it, to turn from the holy commandment delivered unto them.

These people returned to the world, were overcome by its power, and did not seek to restore their relationship to the Lord. Backsliders can return to the Lord through genuine repentance (we just read that in James). But if they stay entangled it would have been better for them never to have known the way of righteousness. In other words, in God's eyes it is better never to have been saved than to receive the gift of eternal life and turn from it permanently.

How could it be better to have never known the way of righteousness? Jude answers this by saying they are "twice dead for whom is reserved the blackness of darkness forever". An eternity of blackest darkness is reserved for them. Those who received Jesus, knew His will, and still walked permanently away will receive the greatest punishment of the second death. Jesus described their torment.

Revelations 2:11 He that hath an ear, let him hear what the Spirit saith unto the churches; He that overcometh shall not be hurt of the second death.

Revelations 20:6 Blessed and holy *is* he that hath part in the first resurrection: on such the second death hath no power, but they shall be priests of God and of Christ, and shall reign with him a thousand years.

Revelations 20:14 And death and hell were cast into the lake of fire. This is the second death.

Revelations 21:8 But the fearful, and unbelieving, and the abominable, and murderers, and whoremongers, and sorcerers, and idolaters, and all liars, shall have their part in the lake which burneth with fire and brimstone: which is the second death.

Luke 12:45-48 But and if that servant say in his heart, My lord delayeth his coming; and shall begin to beat the menservants and maidens, and to eat and drink, and to be drunken; The lord of that servant will come in a day when he looketh not for him, and at an hour when he is not aware, and will cut him in sunder, and will appoint him his portion with the unbelievers. And that servant, which knew his lord's will, and prepared not himself, neither did according to his will, shall be beaten with many stripes. But he that knew not, and did commit things worthy of stripes, shall be beaten with few stripes. For unto whomsoever much is given, of him shall be much required: and to whom men have committed much, of him they will ask the more.

### I NEVER KNEW YOU

A group of individuals who will expect to hear Jesus say enter into heaven but instead will hear Him say, "I never knew you; depart from Me you who practice lawlessness!". It is made up of people who join themselves to Jesus solely for the benefits of salvation. These people follow Jesus at first, but their lack of commitment is ultimately revealed (as in Judas Iscariot).

## Intimacy and Devotion

Matthew 7:22 Many will say to me in that day, Lord, Lord, have we not prophesied in thy name? and in thy name have cast out devils? and in thy name done many wonderful works? And then will I profess unto them, I never knew you: depart from me, ye that work iniquity.

Now we meet the second group of people. These are those who lose their salvation, the ones who at one time knew Him and even did wonders in His name yet did not endure to the end. Jesus also rebuked these people with "I never knew you." How could this be?

Ezekiel 18:24 But when the righteous turneth away from his righteousness, and committeth iniquity, and doeth according to all the abominations that the wicked man doeth, shall he live? All his righteousness that he hath done shall not be mentioned: in his trespass that he hath trespassed, and in his sin that he hath sinned, in them shall he die.

God said He would not remember their righteousness. It would be as if it had never happened. This means He will forget it ever existed. It is as if He never knew this person. This is the reason Jesus will say to those who do not endure to the end, "I never knew you." He will forget their righteousness just as surely as He will forgive and forget the sins of the righteous.

Hebrews 10:16, 17 This *is* the covenant that I will make with them after those days, saith the Lord, I will put my laws into their hearts, and in their minds will I write them; And their sins and iniquities will I remember no more.

God refuses to remember our sins. The devil will, and he accuses us. But God declares, "I have no remembrance of the sins you accuse them of!" In the eyes of God it is as though we have never sinned.

### JUDE'S MAIN POINT

Let's summarize what Jude wanted to say. He urged us to fight earnestly for the faith and described the focus and nature of our battle. The focus is upon those who say they are Christians but only obey God if it is convenient to their self-ruled life. Either they have never been believers, as in the case of Judas, or they have fallen from grace. Whichever the case, they are lukewarm impostors, false brethren, wolves in sheep's clothing, and spots in the church.

Virtually every voice of the New Testament Jesus, Paul, Peter, Jude, and the apostle John warned of those who would fall away. Likewise, I have joined my voice to their warning. Why?

It is the voice of love spoken for the sake of protection! In this we discover the nature of our battle: to keep ourselves and those under our care from falling into the same state as these in disobedience.

After Jude warned of those who would pervert the grace of God, he gave us this strong exhortation of protection:

Jude 1:20, 21 But ye, beloved, building up yourselves on your most holy faith, praying in the Holy Ghost, Keep yourselves in the love of God, looking for the mercy of our Lord Jesus Christ unto eternal life.

We are to keep ourselves in the love of God. Remember, those who love God are obedient to Him. Jude warns of the leaven of disobedience filtering into your life.

1 Corinthians 5:6 Your glorying *is* not good. Know ye not that a little leaven leaveneth the whole lump?

Disobedience is contagious. If you hang around a person with a contagious illness, your own resistance will eventually be worn down, and you will fall prey to it. It is the same with disobedience, but God's words of warning and instruction are like immunization shots. They boost our immunity and resist the virus of disobedience.

Suppose a very contagious disease was spreading throughout your community, but there was also an antidote to prevent the contraction of the disease. Would you immunize your children and teach them preventative health care? Yes, absolutely! We would afford them the protection of the antidote and educate them to prevent the spread of the disease. Even so the Lord and those who penned His Word have gone to great lengths to warn us of the contagious diseases of lukewarmness and disobedience. Listen to the warning given to the elders of Asia:

Acts 20:28-31 Take heed therefore unto yourselves, and to all the flock, over the which the Holy Ghost hath made you overseers, to feed the church of God, which he hath purchased with his own blood. For I know this, that after my departing shall grievous wolves enter in among you, not sparing the flock. Also of your own selves shall men arise, speaking perverse things, to draw away disciples after them. Therefore watch, and remember, that by the space of three years I ceased not to warn every one night and day with tears.

Hear his words, "take heed." It is a warning he repeated night and day, pleading with tears for three years. He wanted to keep his spiritual children from the disease of disobedience. He said that wolves would come in among them. Jesus likened false prophets who come into the church as wolves dressed in sheep's clothing. They talk like Christians but can be discerned by their fruit. Wolves easily enter a flock when the shepherd is not protecting them. Often we want to hear only encouraging and positive messages. However, Paul made it clear that to fully preach the gospel we must warn as well as encourage. By doing this we will present every man perfect in Christ Jesus.

Understanding and obeying the Bible's warnings from God are key elements in the completion of our journey in Christ.

David realized the value of God's precepts. He described them:

Psalms 19:9-11 The fear of the LORD is clean, enduring for ever: the judgments of the LORD are true and righteous altogether. More to be desired are they than gold, yea, than much fine gold: sweeter also than honey and the honeycomb. Moreover by them is thy servant warned: and in keeping of them there is great reward.

To the mature believer the entire counsel of God's Word is sweet, including His warnings. There is a great reward to those who heed them. Ministers are called not only to feed God's sheep but also to protect them. They are to warn of the snares of the enemy. Many ministers have withdrawn from warning their people because they think it is a negative message. It is not negative but preventive it saves lives and churches!

Jesus is certainly not negative, yet He said, "Take heed that no one deceives you". Again He charged His disciples, "Take heed, beware of the leaven of the Pharisees and the leaven of Herod". The contagious leaven of the Pharisees was legalism, which leads to hypocrisy. The contagious leaven of Herod was a disobedient, fleshly lifestyle, which also leads to hypocrisy. These are two contagious diseases that can attack an unaware person and lead them into a disobedient lifestyle.

Peter warned us with,

2 Timothy 3:17 That the man of God may be perfect, throughly furnished unto all good works.

Hear what he is saying. When a person is not warned, he can easily fall away from his steadfast obedience by the error of those who have already fallen.

## LUKEWARM BREEDING GROUNDS

Some of the most difficult places at which to minister are established Christian organizations. Christian schools seem to top the list. These institutions are hard to reach because they are lukewarm breeding grounds for rebellion and disobedience. It may start with a handful of students, often the most established. These young people have grown up in Sunday school and youth group and confess a born-again experience. Yet they are disrespectful to authority, bound by lust, and some have even experimented with drugs or alcohol at a young age. They are obsessed with professional sports figures, Hollywood, dating, and other worldly pursuits. Often they are the sons and daughters of the church leaders, yet they were not trained as children to discern compromise and hypocrisy. This makes them all the more callous and dangerous.

The doctrine of perverted grace begins to permeate their thinking, encouraged by the lascivious lifestyle of others. There is more pressure to conform to the disobedience than to maintain a standard of godliness. Paul explained this dilemma.

1 Corinthians 5:6 Your glorying is not good. Know ye not that a little leaven leaveneth the whole lump?

I have learned that the prophetic anointing of God will arise stronger in the face of hardened people. The harder the people, the stronger the prophetic message. Yet it is for the sake of love and restoration, not for punishment. It often takes a good blow from a sledge hammer to crack a hardened heart. God says, "Is not My word like a hammer that breaks the rock in pieces?"

Jesus is not coming back for a lukewarm bride who fornicates with the world. He is coming for a consecrated bride, unspotted by the world. Would you marry someone who said, "I'll be faithful to you for 364 days a year, but give me one day a year to jump in bed with my old lovers"? Of course not! Neither would Jesus. He is not coming for a bride who has reserved a portion of her heart for the world! Don't be deceived. Don't be contaminated. Don't be infected by the subtlety of disobedience. Do not stray from your steadfast post to be led away to a lukewarm cesspool.

I challenge you to read the Bible in the light of what the Spirit of God has revealed to you through these next two chapters. I realize this message may not have lifted you to a new dimension of happiness, but it holds a wealth of understanding and wisdom that will guard your eternal joy at the possible expense of your temporary happiness. May the grace of our Lord be with you.

# Chapter Seven
## Daily Devotionals

This is to be a help to you. We all need to spend time daily seeking the Lord. Over the next 30 days just use this devotional Chapter one day at a time. A complete devotional to help bring you one step further in your personal journey with the Lord

Just as our physical body needs food for nourishment, our spirit man needs to be fed as well! We all know and understand that a child needs to take in the proper nutrients to grow into strong healthy adults, but many people don't realize that the Word of God is the food that God has given us to strengthen and feed the spiritual part of us. The Bible is the very bread of life that transforms us into who God created us to be. When we are full of His truth, we can grow from spiritual babies into strong men and women of God. I pray that these devotionals will en-courage, uplift you, and that they will increase your appetite for the spiritual food God has given us... His Word!

**Daily Prayer: A prayer to pray daily to help you on your journey**

Father, please help me to see myself as you see me. Your word says that you give me the desires of my heart as I delight myself in you. I desire to feel good about myself, so I can be confident and be a vessel of your blessing here on earth. I thank you that you are helping me to reach my perfect weight in Jesus' name. I thank you that you are teaching me to listen to my body, and to exercise self control in a healthy way. Help me to find an exercise that I can enjoy, and help me to do it in a healthy consistent way. Help me to enjoy healthy foods, and to eat the right portions at the right time of day. Father, I submit myself to you, and resist the devil in every way. I resist wrong foods, and wrong ways of thinking in Jesus name. I am kept in perfect peace in all situations, because I choose to keep my mind on you. Lord, thank you for loving me and empowering me to succeed at reaching my goal weight! I believe that I can do all things through Christ who gives me strength! In Jesus' Name, Amen!

Before you start your devotional journey read this prayer and then allow God to give you your own words to pray for strength every day.

# Day 1:

# Get God Involved

Scripture: 1 Corinthians 10:31 Whether therefore ye eat, or drink, or whatsoever ye do, do all to the glory of God.

Reflection: This verse shows that God truly does care about every area of our lives! In fact, the whole human race was created to glorify God and enjoy Him forever. The fact that we can give glory to God in even our eating and drinking shows that He wants to be involved in this area, and that it is important to Him! It's important to note that giving glory to Him through what we eat is not just about controlling our own eating, because self control is ultimately relying on our self and not God. What it is really about is getting God involved in every area of our lives, even in what and how much we eat. This can be done by asking the Holy Spirit daily to help us in our food choices, to speak to us about when we have had enough, and to also give us the strength to say no to foods that will not bring health to our bodies. When we listen to the Spirit of God on the inside of us regarding what we eat and drink, we are glorifying Him by giving Him access and complete control over these areas in our lives!

# Day 2:

# The Desires of Your Heart

Scripture: Psalms 37:4 Delight thyself also in the LORD; and he shall give thee the desires of thine heart.

Reflection: If we delight ourselves in Him, then our hearts desires would naturally start to line up with His desires for our lives. The dictionary defines the word delight as "To take great pleasure, to satisfy greatly, to please." So, this tells us that when we take great pleasure in our Father, He transforms our heart's desires from the things that temporarily satisfy to His eternal desires.

# Day 3:

# Submit Everything to God

Scripture: Job 22:21 Acquaint now thyself with him, and be at peace: thereby good shall come unto thee.

Reflection: If we submit every area of our life over to God, then we don't need to try and figure things out on our own. We have His guarantee that if we surrender to Him, that things will go well with us. We will have peace knowing that the plans that He has for us are far greater than what we could ever accomplish on our own.

# Day 4:

# Stop the Comparison Game!

Scripture: Galatians 6:4 But let every man prove his own work, and then shall he have rejoicing in himself alone, and not in another.

Reflection: I used to think it was only natural to have thoughts such as, "I wish I had her hair, clothes, body, etc." However, I have found through the Word of God that there are many verses that warn us not to entertain such thoughts. The reason being is that God created each one of us for a unique purpose, and to fulfill something that only we can. He also created each one of us to look, act, and be unique! He created each one of us to be different so that each one of our strengths, gifts, and abilities would come together to form a strong and healthy body. If we are ever going to get our eyes off of other people, then we must make the choice to keep my eyes on what God has given us and use it to the best of our ability. Each time we find ourselves starting to compare ourselves to others, we must make the choice to stop those thoughts in their tracks and remember this verse. When we re-direct our thinking to the truth, we will remember that we were each designed for a unique purpose and have a destiny that no one else can fulfill but us! We must make a choice to focus on the strengths God has given us and do the best we can with what we have in our hands. When we do this, we give glory to God and get the satisfaction of a job well done. Now that sounds way better than walking around feeling jealous any day!

# Day 5:

# Anxious Thoughts

Scripture: Psalms 139:23, 24 Search me, O God, and know my heart: try me, and know my thoughts: And see if *there be any* wicked way in me, and lead me in the way everlasting.

Reflection: No matter where we go, or what we do, (even if it means choosing the wrong path, or hiding from Him), He is there. We can't ever do anything that would cause Him to stop thinking and caring for us! However, when we have anxious thoughts in an area, it offends Him, because it shows that we are not trusting in Him to care for us. This must break His heart considering that He formed us and already has all of our lives planned out. So when we try and fix things ourselves or worry about things, it means we are depending on ourselves. This mindset can eventually take us off the path that God has for us.

# Day 6:

# World Overcoming Faith!

Scripture: 1 John 5:4 For whatsoever is born of God overcometh the world: and this is the victory that overcometh the world, *even* our faith.

Reflection: Just as a butterfly transforms from something that crawls and is earthbound to something that flies and becomes free, so are we transformed into world over-comers when we are children of God. This scripture paints a picture of how when we come to know Christ, we are transformed from a person who is earthbound and bound to natural circumstances, to being able to rise above the circumstances of this world. The second part of this verse explains how to put this overcoming victory into practical application in our lives, which is clearly stated as our faith. When we are simply born of God, and when we put our faith in Him and His promises, then we are promised that we will have world overcoming victory!

# Day 7:

# Heart's Desires

Scripture: 1 Kings 8:58 That he may incline our hearts unto him, to walk in all his ways, and to keep his commandments, and his statutes, and his judgments, which he commanded our fathers.

Reflection: This verse promises us that God will change our desires to conform to His will if we simply ask him to. We can try so hard to do what is right, but how much better it would be if we would simply let God change our very desires from our previous unhealthy ways to His ways that are Higher! We can simply ask God to give us His desires and the desire for life giving foods and healthy amounts of exercise. As we grow in Him, our desires become His.

# Day 8:

# Dealing with Temptation

Scripture: 1 Corinthians 10:13 There hath no temptation taken you but such as is common to man: but God *is* faithful, who will not suffer you to be tempted above that ye are able; but will with the temptation also make a way to escape, that ye may be able to bear *it*.

Reflection: Although being tempted is a reality of living on this earth, this verse tells us that we can be the over-comers that God called us to be in the midst of temptations and trials. In order to find our way out of a tempting situation, we need to look at what is happening when we find ourselves giving into temptation. The place we need to start is first being able to recognize Satan's schemes. Satan is constantly working overtime to get us out of the fruits of the Spirit which are peace, joy, love, gentleness, and self control in order to get us into feelings of fear, doubt, stress, anxiety, etc. When he succeeds in getting us out of the leadership of the Spirit, we start to get into our fleshly nature, which allows us to get over into temptation and sin. The good news is, with the Holy Spirit as our counselor, we don't have to be subject to our flesh any longer. The first step to being over-comers is to ask the Holy Spirit to remind us when we are getting out of peace and make the choice to walk by the Spirit and not get over into the negative emotions of our flesh. When we find that we are getting into worry, doubt, fear, and stress, we need to make the choice to stand firm in His peace, joy, and love. We must continuously make the choice to reign in our emotions and cast our cares over on the Lord.

## Day 9:

## Depend on God's Power!

Scripture: Colossians 1:29 Whereunto I also labour, striving according to his working, which worketh in me mightily.

Reflection: In everything that we do, we should trust, lean, and depend on Christ's mighty power that is at work within us. He has promised to bless whatever it is that we set our hand unto. In order for Him to bless our work, we must take action and put our hand to something. From there, we simply need to rest assured that He is giving us His power (inside of us) to accomplish the task. His Word also promises that we can do ALL things THROUGH Him who gives us strength. These verses combined shows that we don't need to beg and ask God to help us accomplish a goal that we are working towards. Rather, we have his promise that if we do our part (work at something), then He will do His part, (provide the strength and power to reach that goal). When we depend on His power, we can be sure that we will overcome any trial or hardship that may come our way and come out a winner!

# Day 10:

# Abide in His Love

Scripture: John 15:4 Abide in me, and I in you. As the branch cannot bear fruit of itself, except it abide in the vine; no more can ye, except ye abide in me.

Reflection: We see here that the Lord is telling us that in order to bear fruit, we need to abide in Him. He paints a portrait of a vine and a branch. We can see through this illustration that a branch by itself cannot produce fruit unless it receives nourishment from the vine. Therefore, we cannot bear fruit unless we receive nourishment from Him. So how do we abide in Him? The Bible says, "If anyone acknowledges that Jesus is the Son of God, God lives in him and he in God. We know how much God loves us, and we have put our trust in His love. God is love, and all who live in love live in God, and God lives in them." So here we see that we abide in Him by first asking Jesus to be our Lord and Savior, and then put our trust in His love! If we abide in His love then we are abiding in Him! This happens by developing a relationship with Him. As we are poured into by Him, we will be overflowing with His love towards ourselves and others. That is ultimately bearing "fruit"!

# Day 11:

# Rely on His Power!

Scripture: Zechariah 4:6 Then he answered and spake unto me, saying, This *is* the word of the LORD unto Zerubbabel, saying, Not by might, nor by power, but by my spirit, saith the LORD of hosts.

Reflection: I've found that when things in life start to get really busy, hectic, and out of control, then it is then that we have a tendency to try to muster up enough power and might to get through it on our own. Even if we could make it through the tough times on our own strength, why would we want to? This verse clearly tells us where our power source is located... The Spirit of God! The great news is, He lives inside of us! If we simply acknowledge and believe that "We have the same spirit that raised Jesus from the dead living on the inside of us", then our faith will give Him the ability to act in our lives. It is then we can be empowered by Him!

# Day 12:

# God has You on His Mind!

Scripture: Psalms 139:17 How precious also are thy thoughts unto me, O God! how great is the sum of them!

Reflection: What a miracle that the creator of this universe thinks about us. Not only a few thoughts here and there, but a vast sum of them! He cherishes us so much that He has us on His mind all of the time. We are His children, unique and special in every way! How wonderful it would be if we could see ourselves from this point of view. Each one of us is valuable, and God has placed us on this earth at a specific time to fulfill our destiny. On the days that we are tempted to feel unimportant or unworthy of love. This passage of scripture will remind us that we are treasured by Him!

# Day 13:

# Perfect Peace

Scripture: Isaiah 26:3 Thou wilt keep *him* in perfect peace, *whose* mind *is* stayed *on thee:* because he trusteth in thee.

Reflection: What a wonderful promise this is! We have the ability to stay in perfect peace, regardless of our circumstances. So, how do we do this even in the midst of bad situations? This verse shows that perfect peace occurs when we make the choice to do two things. First, we must trust God. Think about it... If you trusted someone to take care of you, provide for you, and guide you, then you would suddenly feel a huge burden lifted off you instantly knowing that someone you trust will take care of what you can't. Next, this verse instructs us to fix our thoughts on Him. We do this by focusing our attention on the Word of God. We must make the choice to reject any thought or emotion that violates God's Word and tell our thoughts and emotions to agree with what God's Word says about us. It is then that we will be world over-comers. We will be able to walk through life with perfect peace as we trust in Him and fix our mind on His promises to us.

# Day 14:

# How Do You See Yourself?

Scripture: Proverbs 23:7 For as he thinketh in his heart, so *is* he: Eat and drink, saith he to thee; but his heart *is* not with thee.

Reflection: This verse is very clear. What we think about ourselves will ultimately become a self-fulfilling prophecy. If we choose to think about who we are in the flesh (or our natural selves without Jesus), we will find shortcomings and failure. If we choose to ponder on these limitations, then it won't take long before we find our life heading in that direction. However, if we choose to think about who we are in Christ, (which is who we truly are and this can be discovered by reading what the Word of God says we are), then we will begin to believe these truths in our hearts. As we believe the truth about who God says we are, we will stand back and watch ourselves becoming all that He said we could be.

# Day 15:

# Experience God's Love

Scripture: Ephesians 3:19 And to know the love of Christ, which passeth knowledge, that ye might be filled with all the fulness of God.

Reflection: God's love towards us is so much more than just an emotion, and it is certainly greater than we could ever understand with our human ability. That's because this world's concept of love is often based on performance. Our society teaches that someone is worthy of love if they are first kind and loving towards you. However, God does not love us based on our performance. He loves us unconditionally, because He is love. So how can we experience His love for us? All we have to do is pray and ask God to give us a revelation of His love so that we would be able to experience it on a daily basis. God wants you to experience His great love so that you are able to be complete with all of the fullness, life, and power that comes from Him. If we find ourselves experiencing anything other than fullness of life, it is possible that we are not experiencing the love of God in our lives. The good news is, all we have to do is ask the Lord for a revelation of His great love for us, and start living a life of fullness and power.

# Day 16:

# Guard Your Heart

Scripture: Proverbs 4:23 Keep thy heart with all diligence; for out of it *are* the issues of life.

Reflection: This verse instructs us to guard our hearts, but it also explains why it is so important! We can see from the Word of God that whatever is in our hearts will determine the course of our lives. Therefore, whatever we put in will come out in one way or another. That is why it is so important to make careful choices as to what we let come into our eyes and ears, because they are the gateway to our hearts. This doesn't mean we need to live isolated from this world, but it does mean that we need to think twice about what we watch, read, and listen to if we want His plans to fully come to pass in our lives. It may seem extreme, but that is why He said His ways are higher than the ways of this world.

# Day 17:

# Don't Be Anxious!

Reflection: When we look around at the world, it is clear that people everywhere are striving after the things that money can buy. This leads to anxiousness as people fight to get to the top and provide and meet their own needs. If we are born again, this verse tells us that we are not to be like the world searching for ways to obtain our provision and care for ourselves. In fact, we see here that these things produce anxiety, and therefore, we are commanded not to seek the things that the rest of the world is striving for. As children of God we are instructed to seek first the Kingdom of God, because it is there that we will be assured that He is our provider and caretaker, and He will give us all that we need.

# Day 18:

# You are Righteous

Scripture: Romans 5:16 And not as *it was* by one that sinned, *so is* the gift: for the judgment *was* by one to condemnation, but the free gift *is* of many offences unto justification.

Reflection: If you are feeling condemned or guilty about a sin you have committed, that feeling is not from the Lord! Even though we may deserve to feel guilty about a wrong that we have done, Jesus died so that we would not get what we deserved! In fact, we can clearly see in this verse that condemnation is tied to Adam's sin. Because Jesus died to redeem us from sin, we are now under the covenant of grace, and completely forgiven! Our right standing with God, (or our righteousness) is a free gift from Jesus to us. Christ is offering this gift to us even in the midst of our sins. We will never deserve or perform our way to a right standing with God. Instead, we must receive the gift He is offering us by faith and believe that we are right before Him because of what Jesus did!

# Day 19:

# Don't Grow Weary!

Scripture: Galatians 6:9 And let us not be weary in well doing: for in due season we shall reap, if we faint not.

Reflection: This verse uses the illustration of sowing and reaping to encourage us during the time of waiting to see a promise come to pass. What an amazing portrait that the Lord painted for us when it comes to the waiting times in our lives! We know in the natural that if we sow something, then we will get a harvest if we take care of the soil properly. This means between the time we plant the seed and see the harvest, we can't go digging up the seed to see if it's doing anything. A plant would never grow that way! It also means that we need to keep the weeds out of the soil, which would choke and starve the seed. God cares and worries of this life come and choke the Word out of our hearts. We know that worrying can stop the harvest of what we are believing for. In order to reap a harvest of the promise we are standing on (which is the seed), we need to plant the seed, and let God work. After all, He can make a huge oak tree grow from one little seed! No human ability could ever do that! Don't grow weary while doing good, for you will reap your harvest in due season if you don't give up!

# Day 20:

# Understanding His Love

Scripture: 1 Corinthians 13:13 And now abideth faith, hope, charity, these three; but the greatest of these *is* charity.

Reflection: Here we see that faith, hope, and love are eternal things. Just knowing this means that we should pay careful attention to them because the Bible instructs us to keep our mind on eternal things. This verse also explains that love is greater than hope and faith. The reason being is because neither of these things (faith or hope) will work without first knowing God's love for us. The Bible confirms that "Faith works by love". This makes perfect sense if we think about it. How could we believe that someone would fulfill their promise to us, (which is essentially what faith and hope are) unless we first knew that they loved us? So, if you find yourself struggling to have hope or faith in a certain area, choose to focus on the greatest thing, which is God's love for you, and you will find that these other eternal things will come to you as well.

# Day 21:

# You Are an Overcomer!

Scripture: 1 John 4:4 Ye are of God, little children, and have overcome them: because greater is he that is in you, than he that is in the world.

Reflection: If we have received Jesus as our Savior, then we are children of God. According to this verse, if we are His children, then we are already over-comers! When we ask Jesus to come into our hearts and be Lord of our lives, He comes to live inside of us. When this happens, it is truly a miracle! Think of it, the creator of the universe comes to live inside of you and me! So, we must ask ourselves, is there anything that God can't overcome? Is there any disease, any emotional discouragement, any trial that is too great for God to handle? The answer is a resounding NO! So, what does that mean for His children? It means that because He lives on the inside of us, we are able to overcome anything in this world! It's time that we start believing this scripture and take it as a personal truth. We must begin to see ourselves as victors and over-comers, because In Christ we are able to overcome everything in this world. We can do ALL things through Christ who lives in us! Praise God!

# Day 22:

# The Power of Our Words

Scripture: Proverbs 18:21 Death and life *are* in the power of the tongue: and they that love it shall eat the fruit thereof.

Reflection: God created the heavens, the earth, and everything in the world by His words. We were created in the image of God, which means that our words, when spoken in faith, have the power to produce as well. By this verse we can see that there is no such things as words that don't have meaning. Each word we speak will either produce life or death. The Bible has so much to say about the power of our words. When we speak the Word of God in faith, it can be one of our most powerful weapons against the devil. The Bible also says that faith-filled words can move mountains. We also see that the authority in the spoken Word was faith that made Jesus marvel. If we begin to speak words in faith that line up with God's Word, then we will have the positive results that follow. But if we continue to speak words of doubt, we will eventually believe them and have the negative things that these words produce. Death and life are in the power of every word we speak.

# Day 23:

# The Importance of The Word

Scripture: Proverbs 4:20-22 My son, attend to my words; incline thine ear unto my sayings. Let them not depart from thine eyes; keep them in the midst of thine heart. For they *are* life unto those that find them, and health to all their flesh.

Reflection: God revealed to me that in order for us to find true health for our whole body, we have to keep the Word of God and what He said about us constantly before our eyes. I started looking up scriptures and asked God to give me hope for things that I was believing for. One practical way that we can do this is by writing scriptures on note cards and putting them wherever we can keep them in front of our eyes. This will also play a crucial role in renewing our mind, because we are able to combat the lies of this world with the truth of God's Word. It eventually became much easier to keep the truth of what we are believing for in the forefront of our mind as it gets rooted deep in our hearts. It won't take long before we begin to believe what He said about us more than what we are experiencing in our circumstances. When we keep our eyes on the Word we will begin to see ourselves as the healthy, balanced, and whole person that God created us to be!

# Day 24:

# Fear of the Lord

Scripture: Proverbs 3:9 Honour the LORD with thy substance, and with the firstfruits of all thine increase:

Reflection: Many times the word fear is associated with a negative emotion. However, when the Bible tells us to fear the Lord it is referring to something completely different. In fact, this type of fear is not an emotion at all, but it is an action. The fear of the Lord is an act of reverence and honor towards Him. This action takes place on our part when we first recognize that He alone is God. When we acknowledge that He knows better than we do and that ultimately His ways are higher than ours, then we can submit freely to His leading knowing that He is Lord of all. This scripture promises that when we come to a place of humility, choosing to do things His way, then we will have healing in every broken place in our lives, restoration, and strength that can only come from Him.

# Day 25:

# Lay Your Burdens Down

Scripture: Psalms 55:22 Cast thy burden upon the LORD, and he shall sustain thee: he shall never suffer the righteous to be moved.

Reflection: The first and most important step in giving something to God is to trust Him to take care of what He has promised to take care of. If we make the decision to pray about something, then we must also make the decision to give the burden of that thing over to the Lord. However, if we find ourselves still worrying about something that we originally gave to the Lord, then it is most likely because we have tried to take it back and deal with it on our own. We must recognize that He has promised to take care of us, guide us, and provide for us. If we choose to focus on these promises, then we can release the cares of these things once and for all over to Him. If we find ourselves worrying about that thing again, then we must make the choice to stop those anxious thoughts right in their tracks and say, "No, I refuse to worry about this thing anymore because God is taking care of it!" He promises that if we do this, that His peace that passes all understanding will flood our mind as we put our trust in Him.

# Day 26:

# Nothing for God is Wasted

Scripture: 1 Corinthians 15:58 Therefore, my beloved brethren, be ye stedfast, unmoveable, always abounding in the work of the Lord, forasmuch as ye know that your labour is not in vain in the Lord.

Reflection: As long as we are working for the Lord, then nothing we do, big or small, could ever be wasted. This is so important to remember in a society where success is measured by status, wealth, position, and appearance. When we find ourselves striving to do more or feel that we are not doing anything of importance, it is then that we need to remind ourselves of this truth. If we go about our daily tasks with a mindset of serving the Lord with enthusiasm, then we are doing something useful and ultimately He is pleased with us.

# Day 27:

# Renewing Your Mind

Scripture: Romans 12:2 And be not conformed to this world: but be ye transformed by the renewing of your mind, that ye may prove what *is* that good, and acceptable, and perfect, will of God.

Reflection: Have you believed a lie in some area of your life? Lies can come in the form of a person saying something, or even in your own internal thoughts. If we have received anything less than what God promises in His Word, which is ABUNDANT life, then there is a chance we have believed a lie in some area of our life. We must begin to recognize the source of lies. The Bible says that Satan is the father of lies, and refuse to take it anymore! Once we recognize areas that we have believed lies, we are then able to renew our minds with the truth of the Word of God. It is that knowledge of truth that ultimately sets us free. God will do a good work in each one of us and change us from the inside out as we pursue and seek His will for our lives. There is an enemy that is real, and he comes to steal kill and destroy us. He does this by planting lies into our lives. But the good new is, Jesus came so we could have abundant life! Let God renew your mind with His truth and begin to believe what He says about you starting today. The only thing standing in the way between the plans Satan has for us and the abundant life Jesus provided, is our choice to surrender everything to Him and renew your mind with the truth of the Word of God.

# Day 28:

# The Importance of Prayer

Scripture: Romans 12:12 Rejoicing in hope; patient in tribulation; continuing instant in prayer;

Reflection: This verse encourages us to be faithful and persistent in prayer because it is our access to God for a life of spiritual intimacy and power. It is also the means by which God advances His kingdom and purposes here on this earth through us!

# Day 29:

# The Unfailing Love of God

Scripture: Romans 8:39 Nor height, nor depth, nor any other creature, shall be able to separate us from the love of God, which is in Christ Jesus our Lord.

Reflection: I know we have all heard the saying "Jesus loves You" more times than we can count, but we need to have more than just a knowledge of this truth. What we really need is a revelation of how deep His love is for us! This saying must become more than just a bumper sticker or a cliché saying used to make someone's day brighter. We need to have a deep understanding that the very creator of this universe loves each one of us so much that He calls us by name! The Bible says, before we were even born, He knew us. He created each one of us in our mother's womb and He has a plan and purpose for each of one of us. He cares about every detail of our lives. He said that He knows the number of hairs on our head. There may be days that it is hard to believe the love that He has for us. This can happen for a number of reasons. Maybe something has happened that makes us question if He still loves us or maybe we just don't "feel" His love. Although this is common, nothing can separate us from His love...not emotions, not circumstances, or our actions. Nothing! I truly believe that it will take a lifetime for us to even begin to understand the great depth, height, and length of God's love for us. The greatest act of love that has or ever will be displayed is when God sent his only Son to die for you and I so we could have a close, intimate relationship with Him. Nothing can or ever will change that act of love He demonstrated for you.

# Day 30:

# You Must Believe!

Scripture: John 16:31 Jesus answered them, Do ye now believe?

Reflection: This passage of scripture is referring to when Jesus was talking to his disciples. He had spent so much time with His disciples trying to get them to believe everything that He was telling them, but there finally came a point when they simply had to use what they learned and just believe! In order to be truly successful at anything we plan to accomplish, we must take God at His Word, and simply choose to believe His promises!

Use these scriptures to gain further revelation of God's promises. These scriptures can be used to read, confess, declare, and to renew your mind daily.

One of the most important things we can do is to discover our true identity in Christ and see ourselves through Jesus' eyes. One way we can do this is by believing and speaking out the truth of what God says about us in His word. Here are just some of the many scriptures that reflect who we are in Christ. I encourage you to speak them out over yourself daily until you have a renewed mind in this area and gain a revelation of your identity in Him.

I am adopted as his child

Ephesians 1:5 Having predestinated us unto the adoption of children by Jesus Christ to himself, according to the good pleasure of his will,

I am a member of Christ's Body

1 Corinthians 12:27 Now ye are the body of Christ, and members in particular.

I am confident that God will perfect the work He has begun in me

Philippians 1:6 Being confident of this very thing, that he which hath begun a good work in you will perform *it* until the day of Jesus Christ:

I have not been given a spirit of fear, but of power, love and self-discipline

2 Timothy 1:7 For God hath not given us the spirit of fear; but of power, and of love, and of a sound mind.

### I am born of God and the evil one cannot touch me

1 John 5:18 We know that whosoever is born of God sinneth not; but he that is begotten of God keepeth himself, and that wicked one toucheth him not.

### I am blessed with every spiritual blessing

Ephesians 1:3 Blessed *be* the God and Father of our Lord Jesus Christ, who hath blessed us with all spiritual blessings in heavenly *places* in Christ:

### I am chosen before the creation of the world. I am holy and blameless

Ephesians 1:4 According as he hath chosen us in him before the foundation of the world, that we should be holy and without blame before him in love:

Ephesians 1:11 In whom also we have obtained an inheritance, being predestinated according to the purpose of him who worketh all things after the counsel of his own will:

### I am forgiven

Ephesians 1:8 Wherein he hath abounded toward us in all wisdom and prudence;

Colossians 1:14 In whom we have redemption through his blood, *even* the forgiveness of sins:

### I have purpose

Ephesians 1:9 Having made known unto us the mystery of his will, according to his good pleasure which he hath purposed in himself:

Ephesians 3:11 According to the eternal purpose which he purposed in Christ Jesus our Lord:

### I am God's workmanship

Ephesians 2:10 For we are his workmanship, created in Christ Jesus unto good works, which God hath before ordained that we should walk in them.

## Intimacy and Devotion

### I have peace

Ephesians 2:14 For he is our peace, who hath made both one, and hath broken down the middle wall of partition *between us;*

### I am secure

Ephesians 2:20 And are built upon the foundation of the apostles and prophets, Jesus Christ himself being the chief corner *stone;*

### I am a holy temple

Ephesians 2:21 In whom all the building fitly framed together groweth unto an holy temple in the Lord:

1 Corinthians 6:19 What? know ye not that your body is the temple of the Holy Ghost *which is* in you, which ye have of God, and ye are not your own?

### I am a dwelling for the Holy Spirit

Ephesians 2:22 In whom ye also are builded together for an habitation of God through the Spirit.

### God's power works through me

Ephesians 3:7 Whereof I was made a minister, according to the gift of the grace of God given unto me by the effectual working of his power.

I can approach God with freedom and confidence

Ephesians 3:12 In whom we have boldness and access with confidence by the faith of him.

I can grasp how wide, long, high and deep Christ's love is

Ephesians 3:18 May be able to comprehend with all saints what *is* the breadth, and length, and depth, and height;

I can bring glory to God

Ephesians 3:21 Unto him *be* glory in the church by Christ Jesus throughout all ages, world without end. Amen.

I have been called

Ephesians 4:1, 2 I therefore, the prisoner of the Lord, beseech you that ye walk worthy of the vocation wherewith ye are called, With all lowliness and meekness, with longsuffering, forbearing one another in love;

1 Timothy 1:9 Knowing this, that the law is not made for a righteous man, but for the lawless and disobedient, for the ungodly and for sinners, for unholy and profane, for murderers of fathers and murderers of mothers, for manslayers,

I can be kind and compassionate to others

&

I can forgive others

Ephesians 4:32 And be ye kind one to another, tenderhearted, forgiving one another, even as God for Christ's sake hath forgiven you.

I am a light to others, and can exhibit goodness, righteousness and truth

Ephesians 5:8, 9 For ye were sometimes darkness, but now *are ye* light in the Lord: walk as children of light: (For the fruit of the Spirit *is* in all goodness and righteousness and truth;)

I am not alone

Hebrews 13:5 *Let your* conversation *be* without covetousness; *and be* content with such things as ye have:

for he hath said, I will never leave thee, nor forsake thee.

### I possess the mind of Christ

1 Corinthians 2:16 For who hath known the mind of the Lord, that he may instruct him? But we have the mind of Christ.

### I am victorious

1 John 5:4 For whatsoever is born of God overcometh the world: and this is the victory that overcometh the world, *even* our faith.

### My heart and mind is protected with God's peace

Philippians 4:7 And the peace of God, which passeth all understanding, shall keep your hearts and minds through Christ Jesus.

### I am chosen and dearly loved

Colossians 3:12 Put on therefore, as the elect of God, holy and beloved, bowels of mercies, kindness, humbleness of mind, meekness, longsuffering;

### I am protected

John 10:28 And I give unto them eternal life; and they shall never perish, neither shall any *man* pluck them out of my hand.

### I am a new creation

2 Corinthians 5:17 Therefore if any man *be* in Christ, *he is* a new creature: old things are passed away; behold, all things are become new.

# Chapter Eight
## Daily Bible Reading

Spend time every day reading the Bible. I have listed many scriptures that will help you in your walk with the Lord.

Revelations 3:20 Behold, I stand at the door, and knock: if any man hear my voice, and open the door, I will come in to him, and will sup with him, and he with me.

John 15:7 If ye abide in me, and my words abide in you, ye shall ask what ye will, and it shall be done unto you.

Romans 5:1-21 Therefore being justified by faith, we have peace with God through our Lord Jesus Christ: By whom also we have access by faith into this grace wherein we stand, and rejoice in hope of the glory of God. And not only *so*, but we glory in tribulations also: knowing that tribulation worketh patience; And patience, experience; and experience, hope: And hope maketh not ashamed; because the love of God is shed abroad in our hearts by the Holy Ghost which is given unto us. For when we were yet without strength, in due time Christ died for the ungodly. For scarcely for a righteous man will one die: yet peradventure for a good man some would even dare to die. But God commendeth his love toward us, in that, while we were yet sinners, Christ died for us. Much more then, being now justified by his blood, we shall be saved from wrath through him. For if, when we were enemies, we were reconciled to God by the death of his Son, much more, being reconciled, we shall be saved by his life. And not only *so*, but we also joy in God through our Lord Jesus Christ, by whom we have now received the atonement. Wherefore, as by one man sin entered into the world, and death by sin; and so death passed upon all men, for that all have sinned: (For until the law sin was in the world: but sin is not imputed when there is no law. Nevertheless death reigned from Adam to Moses, even over them that had not sinned after the similitude of Adam's transgression, who is the figure of him that was to come. But not as the offence, so also *is* the free gift. For if through the offence of one many be dead, much more the grace of God, and the gift by grace, *which is* by one man, Jesus Christ, hath abounded unto many. And not as *it was* by one that sinned, *so is* the gift: for the judgment *was* by one to condemnation, but the free gift *is* of many offences unto justification. For if by one man's offence death reigned by one; much more they which receive abundance of grace and of the gift of righteousness shall reign in life by one, Jesus Christ.) Therefore as by the offence of one *judgment came* upon all men to condemnation; even so by the righteousness of one *the free gift came* upon all men unto justification of life. For as by one man's disobedience many were made sinners, so by the obedience of one shall many be made righteous. Moreover the law entered, that the offence might abound. But where sin abounded, grace did much more abound: That as sin hath reigned unto death, even so might grace reign through righteousness unto eternal life by Jesus Christ our Lord.

Matthew 6:5-24 And when thou prayest, thou shalt not be as the hypocrites *are:* for they love to pray standing in the synagogues and in the corners of the streets, that they may be seen of men. Verily I say unto you, They have their reward. But thou, when thou prayest, enter into thy closet, and when thou hast shut thy door, pray to thy Father which is in secret; and thy Father which seeth in secret shall reward thee openly. But when ye pray, use not vain repetitions, as the heathen *do:* for they think that they shall be heard for their much speaking. Be not ye therefore like unto them: for your Father knoweth what things ye have need of, before ye ask him. After this manner therefore pray ye: Our Father which art in heaven, Hallowed be thy name. Thy kingdom come. Thy will be done in earth, as *it is* in heaven. Give us this day our daily bread. And forgive us our debts, as we forgive our debtors. And lead us not into temptation, but deliver us from evil: For thine is the kingdom, and the power, and the glory, for ever. Amen. For if ye forgive men their trespasses, your heavenly Father will also forgive you: But if ye forgive not men their trespasses, neither will your Father forgive your trespasses. Moreover when ye fast, be not, as the hypocrites, of a sad countenance: for they disfigure their faces, that they may appear unto men to fast. Verily I say unto you, They have their reward. But thou, when thou fastest, anoint thine head, and wash thy face; That thou appear not unto men to fast, but unto thy Father which is in secret: and thy Father, which seeth in secret, shall reward thee openly. Lay not up for yourselves treasures upon earth, where moth and rust doth corrupt, and where thieves break through and steal: But lay up for yourselves treasures in heaven, where neither moth nor rust doth corrupt, and where thieves do not break through nor steal: For where your treasure is, there will your heart be also. The light of the body is the eye: if therefore thine eye be single, thy whole body shall be full of light. But if thine eye be evil, thy whole body shall be full of darkness. If therefore the light that is in thee be darkness, how great *is* that darkness! No man can serve two masters: for either he will hate the one, and love the other; or else he will hold to the one, and despise the other. Ye cannot serve God and mammon.

2 Timothy 2:21 If a man therefore purge himself from these, he shall be a vessel unto honour, sanctified, and meet for the master's use, *and* prepared unto every good work.

Psalms 139:1-24 To the chief Musician, A Psalm of David. O LORD, thou hast searched me, and known *me*. Thou knowest my downsitting and mine uprising, thou understandest my thought afar off. Thou compassest my path and my lying down, and art acquainted *with* all my ways. For *there is* not a word in my tongue, *but,* lo, O LORD, thou knowest it altogether. Thou hast beset me behind and before, and laid thine hand upon me. *Such* knowledge *is* too wonderful for me; it is high, I cannot *attain* unto it. Whither shall I go from thy spirit? or whither shall I flee from thy presence? If I ascend up into heaven, thou *art* there: if I make my bed in hell, behold, thou *art there. If* I take the wings of the morning, *and* dwell in the uttermost parts of the sea; Even there shall thy hand lead me, and thy right hand shall hold me. If I say, Surely the darkness shall cover me; even the night shall be light about me. Yea, the darkness hideth not from thee; but the night shineth as the day: the darkness and the light *are* both alike *to thee.* For thou hast possessed my reins: thou hast covered me in my mother's womb. I will praise thee; for I am fearfully *and* wonderfully made: marvellous *are* thy works; and *that* my soul knoweth right well. My substance was not hid from thee, when I was made in secret, *and* curiously wrought in the lowest parts of the earth. Thine eyes did see my substance, yet being unperfect; and in thy book all *my members* were written, *which* in continuance were fashioned, when *as yet there was* none of them. How precious also are thy thoughts unto me, O God! how great is the sum of them! *If* I should count them, they are more in number than the sand: when I awake, I am still with thee. Surely thou wilt slay the wicked, O God: depart from me therefore, ye bloody men.

For they speak against thee wickedly, *and* thine enemies take *thy name* in vain. Do not I hate them, O LORD, that hate thee? and am not I grieved with those that rise up against thee? I hate them with perfect hatred: I count them mine enemies. Search me, O God, and know my heart: try me, and know my thoughts: And see if *there be any* wicked way in me, and lead me in the way everlasting.

Romans 7:1-5 Know ye not, brethren, (for I speak to them that know the law,) how that the law hath dominion over a man as long as he liveth? For the woman which hath an husband is bound by the law to *her* husband so long as he liveth; but if the husband be dead, she is loosed from the law of *her* husband. So then if, while *her* husband liveth, she be married to another man, she shall be called an adulteress: but if her husband be dead, she is free from that law; so that she is no adulteress, though she be married to another man. Wherefore, my brethren, ye also are become dead to the law by the body of Christ; that ye should be married to another, *even* to him who is raised from the dead, that we should bring forth fruit unto God. For when we were in the flesh, the motions of sins, which were by the law, did work in our members to bring forth fruit unto death.

Psalms 23:1-6 A Psalm of David. The LORD *is* my shepherd; I shall not want. He maketh me to lie down in green pastures: he leadeth me beside the still waters. He restoreth my soul: he leadeth me in the paths of righteousness for his name's sake. Yea, though I walk through the valley of the shadow of death, I will fear no evil: for thou *art* with me; thy rod and thy staff they comfort me. Thou preparest a table before me in the presence of mine enemies: thou anointest my head with oil; my cup runneth over. Surely goodness and mercy shall follow me all the days of my life: and I will dwell in the house of the LORD for ever.

Psalms 119:1-176 ALEPH. Blessed *are* the undefiled in the way, who walk in the law of the LORD. Blessed *are* they that keep his testimonies, *and that* seek him with the whole heart. They also do no iniquity: they walk in his ways. Thou hast commanded *us* to keep thy precepts diligently. O that my ways were directed to keep thy statutes! Then shall I not be ashamed, when I have respect unto all thy commandments. I will praise thee with uprightness of heart, when I shall have learned thy righteous judgments. I will keep thy statutes: O forsake me not utterly. BETH. Wherewithal shall a young man cleanse his way? by taking heed *thereto* according to thy word. With my whole heart have I sought thee: O let me not wander from thy commandments. Thy word have I hid in mine heart, that I might not sin against thee. Blessed *art* thou, O LORD: teach me thy statutes. With my lips have I declared all the judgments of thy mouth. I have rejoiced in the way of thy testimonies, as *much as* in all riches. I will meditate in thy precepts, and have respect unto thy ways. I will delight myself in thy statutes: I will not forget thy word. GIMEL. Deal bountifully with thy servant, *that* I may live, and keep thy word. Open thou mine eyes, that I may behold wondrous things out of thy law. I *am* a stranger in the earth: hide not thy commandments from me. My soul breaketh for the longing *that it hath* unto thy judgments at all times. Thou hast rebuked the proud *that are* cursed, which do err from thy commandments. Remove from me reproach and contempt; for I have kept thy testimonies. Princes also did sit *and* speak against me: *but* thy servant did meditate in thy statutes. Thy testimonies also *are* my delight *and* my counsellors. DALETH. My soul cleaveth unto the dust: quicken thou me according to thy word. I have declared my ways, and thou heardest me: teach me thy statutes. Make me to understand the way of thy precepts: so shall I talk of thy wondrous works. My soul melteth for heaviness: strengthen thou me according unto thy word. Remove from me the way of lying: and grant me thy law graciously. I have chosen the way of truth: thy judgments have I laid *before me.* I have stuck unto thy testimonies: O LORD, put me not to shame. I will run the way of thy commandments, when thou shalt enlarge my heart. HE. Teach me, O LORD, the way of thy statutes; and I shall keep it *unto* the end. Give me understanding, and I shall keep thy law; yea, I shall observe it with *my* whole heart. Make me to go in the path of thy commandments; for therein do I delight. Incline my heart unto thy testimonies, and not to covetousness. Turn away mine eyes from beholding vanity; *and* quicken thou me in thy way. Stablish thy word unto thy servant, who *is devoted* to thy fear. Turn away my reproach which I fear: for thy judgments *are* good. Behold, I have longed after thy precepts: quicken me in thy righteousness. Let thy mercies come also unto me, O LORD, *even* thy salvation, according to thy word. So shall I have wherewith to answer him that reproacheth me: for I trust in thy word. And take not the word of truth utterly out of my mouth; for I have hoped in thy judgments. So shall I keep thy law continually for ever and ever. And I will walk at liberty: for I seek thy precepts. I will speak of thy testimonies also before kings, and will not be ashamed. And I will delight myself in thy commandments, which I have loved. My hands also will I lift up unto thy commandments, which I have loved; and I will meditate in thy statutes. Remember the word unto thy servant, upon which thou hast caused me to hope. This *is* my comfort in my affliction: for thy word hath quickened me. The proud have had me greatly in derision: *yet* have I not declined from thy law. I remembered thy judgments of old, O LORD; and have comforted myself. Horror hath taken hold upon me because of the wicked that forsake thy law. Thy statutes have been my songs in the house of my pilgrimage. I have remembered thy name, O LORD, in the night, and have kept thy law. This I had, because I kept thy precepts. *Thou art* my portion, O LORD: I have said that I would keep thy words. I intreated thy favour with *my* whole heart: be merciful unto me according to thy word. I thought on my ways, and turned my feet unto thy testimonies. I made haste, and delayed not to keep thy commandments. The bands of the wicked have robbed me: *but* I have not forgotten thy law. At midnight I will rise to give thanks unto thee because of thy righteous judgments. I *am* a companion of all *them* that fear thee, and of them that keep thy precepts. The earth, O LORD, is full of thy mercy: teach me thy statutes. Thou hast dealt well with thy servant, O LORD, according unto thy word. Teach me good judgment and knowledge: for I have believed thy commandments. Before I was afflicted I went astray: but now have I kept thy word. Thou *art* good, and doest good; teach me thy statutes. The proud have forged a lie against me: *but* I will keep thy precepts with *my* whole heart. Their heart is as fat as grease; *but* I delight in thy law. *It is* good for me that I have been afflicted; that I might learn thy statutes. The law of thy mouth *is* better unto me than thousands of gold and silver. Thy hands have made me and fashioned me: give me understanding, that I may learn thy commandments. They that fear thee will be glad when they see me; because I have hoped in thy word. I know, O LORD, that thy judgments *are* right, and *that* thou in faithfulness hast afflicted me. Let, I pray thee, thy merciful kindness be for my comfort, according to thy word unto thy servant. Let thy tender mercies come unto me, that I may live: for thy law *is* my delight. Let the proud be ashamed; for they dealt perversely with me without a cause: *but* I will meditate in thy precepts. Let those that fear thee turn unto me, and those that have known thy testimonies. Let my heart be sound in thy statutes; that I be not ashamed. My soul fainteth for thy salvation: *but* I hope in thy word. Mine eyes fail for thy word, saying, When wilt thou comfort me? For I am become like a bottle in the smoke; *yet* do I not forget thy statutes. How many *are* the days of thy servant? when wilt thou execute judgment on them that persecute me? The proud have digged pits for me, which *are* not after thy law. All thy commandments *are* faithful: they persecute me wrongfully; help thou me. They had almost consumed me upon earth; but I forsook not thy precepts. Quicken me after thy lovingkindness; so shall I keep the testimony of thy mouth. For ever, O LORD, thy word is settled in heaven. Thy faithfulness *is* unto all generations: thou hast established the earth, and it abideth. They continue this day according to thine ordinances: for all *are* thy servants. Unless thy law *had been* my delights, I should then have perished in mine affliction. I will never forget thy precepts: for with them thou hast quickened me. I *am* thine, save me; for I have sought thy precepts. The wicked have waited for me to destroy me: *but* I will consider thy testimonies. I have seen an end of all perfection: *but* thy commandment *is* exceeding broad. O how love I thy law! it *is* my meditation all the day. Thou through thy commandments hast made me wiser than mine enemies: for they *are* ever with me. I have more understanding than all my teachers: for thy testimonies *are* my meditation. I understand more than the ancients, because I keep thy precepts. I have refrained my feet from every evil way, that I might keep thy word. I have not departed from thy judgments: for thou hast taught me. How sweet are thy words unto my taste! *yea, sweeter* than honey to my mouth! Through thy precepts I get understanding: therefore I hate every false way. Thy word *is* a lamp unto my feet, and a light unto my path. I have sworn, and I will perform *it,* that I will keep thy righteous judgments. I am afflicted very much: quicken me, O LORD, according unto thy word. Accept, I beseech thee, the freewill offerings of my mouth, O LORD, and teach me thy judgments. My soul *is* continually in my hand: yet do I not forget thy law. The wicked have laid a snare for me: yet I erred not from thy precepts. Thy testimonies have I taken as an heritage for ever: for they *are* the rejoicing of my heart. I have inclined mine heart to perform thy statutes alway, *even unto* the end. I hate *vain* thoughts: but thy law do I love. Thou *art* my hiding place and my shield: I hope in thy word. Depart from me, ye evildoers: for I will keep the commandments of my God. Uphold me according unto thy word, that I may live: and let me not be ashamed of my hope. Hold thou me up, and I shall be safe: and I will have respect unto thy statutes continually. Thou hast trodden down all them that err from thy statutes: for their deceit *is* falsehood. Thou puttest away all the wicked of the earth *like* dross: therefore I love thy testimonies. My flesh trembleth for fear of thee; and I am afraid of thy judgments. I have done judgment and justice: leave me not to mine oppressors. Be surety for thy servant for good: let not the proud oppress me. Mine eyes fail for thy salvation, and for the word of thy righteousness. Deal with thy servant according unto thy mercy, and teach me thy statutes. I *am* thy servant; give me understanding, that I may know thy testimonies. *It is* time for *thee,* LORD, to work: *for* they have made void thy law. Therefore I love thy commandments above gold; yea, above fine gold. Therefore I esteem all *thy* precepts *concerning* all *things to be* right; *and* I hate every false way. Thy testimonies *are* wonderful: therefore doth my soul keep them. The entrance of thy words giveth light; it giveth understanding unto the simple. I opened my mouth, and panted: for I longed for thy commandments. Look thou upon me, and be merciful unto me, as thou usest to do unto those that love thy name. Order my steps in thy word: and let not any iniquity have dominion over me. Deliver me from the oppression of man: so will I keep thy precepts. Make thy face to shine upon thy servant; and teach me thy statutes. Rivers of waters run down mine eyes, because they keep not thy law. Righteous *art* thou, O LORD, and upright *are* thy judgments. Thy testimonies *that* thou hast commanded *are* righteous and very faithful. My zeal hath consumed me, because mine enemies have forgotten thy words. Thy word *is* very pure: therefore thy servant loveth it. I *am* small and despised: *yet* do not I forget thy precepts. Thy righteousness *is* an everlasting righteousness, and thy law *is* the truth. Trouble and anguish have taken hold on me: *yet* thy commandments *are* my delights. The righteousness of thy testimonies *is* everlasting: give me understanding, and I shall live. I cried with *my* whole heart; hear me, O LORD: I will keep thy statutes. I cried unto thee; save me, and I shall keep thy testimonies. I prevented the dawning of the morning, and cried: I hoped in thy word. Mine eyes prevent the *night* watches, that I might meditate in thy word. Hear my voice according unto thy lovingkindness: O LORD, quicken me according to thy judgment. They draw nigh that follow after mischief: they are far from thy law. Thou *art* near, O LORD; and all thy commandments *are* truth. Concerning thy testimonies, I have known of old that thou hast founded them for ever. Consider mine affliction, and deliver me: for I do not forget thy law. Plead my cause, and deliver me: quicken me according to thy word. Salvation *is* far from the wicked: for they seek not thy statutes. Great *are* thy tender mercies, O LORD: quicken me according to thy judgments. Many *are* my persecutors and mine enemies; *yet* do I not decline from thy testimonies. I beheld the transgressors, and was grieved; because they kept not thy word. Consider how I love thy precepts: quicken me, O LORD, according to thy lovingkindness. Thy word *is* true *from* the beginning: and every one of thy righteous judgments *endureth* for ever. SCHIN. Princes have persecuted me without a cause: but my heart standeth in awe of thy word. I rejoice at thy word, as one that findeth great spoil. I hate and abhor lying: *but* thy law do I love. Seven times a day do I praise thee because of thy righteous judgments. Great peace have they which love thy law: and nothing shall offend them. LORD, I have hoped for thy salvation, and done thy commandments. My soul hath kept thy testimonies; and I love them exceedingly. I have kept thy precepts and thy testimonies: for all my ways *are* before thee. TAU. Let my cry come near before thee, O LORD: give me understanding according to thy word. Let my supplication come before thee: deliver me according to thy word. My lips shall utter praise, when thou hast taught me thy statutes. My tongue shall speak of thy word: for all thy commandments *are* righteousness. Let thine hand help me; for I have chosen thy precepts. I have longed for thy salvation, O LORD; and thy law *is* my delight. Let my soul live, and it shall praise thee; and let thy judgments help me. I have gone astray like a lost sheep; seek thy servant; for I do not forget thy commandments.

Psalms 91:16 With long life will I satisfy him, and shew him my salvation.

1 Peter 4:10 As every man hath received the gift, *even so* minister the same one to another, as good stewards of the manifold grace of God.

Philippians 4:8 Finally, brethren, whatsoever things are true, whatsoever things *are* honest, whatsoever things *are* just, whatsoever things *are* pure, whatsoever things *are* lovely, whatsoever things *are* of good report; if *there be* any virtue, and if *there be* any praise, think on these things.

Psalms 145:20 The LORD preserveth all them that love him: but all the wicked will he destroy.

Hebrews 11:1-40 Now faith is the substance of things hoped for, the evidence of things not seen. For by it the elders obtained a good report. Through faith we understand that the worlds were framed by the word of God, so that things which are seen were not made of things which do appear. By faith Abel offered unto God a more excellent sacrifice than Cain, by which he obtained witness that he was righteous, God testifying of his gifts: and by it he being dead yet speaketh. By faith Enoch was translated that he should not see death; and was not found, because God had translated him: for before his translation he had this testimony, that he pleased God. But without faith *it is* impossible to please *him:* for he that cometh to God must believe that he is, and *that* he is a rewarder of them that diligently seek him. By faith Noah, being warned of God of things not seen as yet, moved with fear, prepared an ark to the saving of his house; by the which he condemned the world, and became heir of the righteousness which is by faith. By faith Abraham, when he was called to go out into a place which he should after receive for an inheritance, obeyed; and he went out, not knowing whither he went. By faith he sojourned in the land of promise, as *in* a strange country, dwelling in tabernacles with Isaac and Jacob, the heirs with him of the same promise: For he looked for a city which hath foundations, whose builder and maker *is* God. Through faith also Sara herself received strength to conceive seed, and was delivered of a child when she was past age, because she judged him faithful who had promised. Therefore sprang there even of one, and him as good as dead, *so many* as the stars of the sky in multitude, and as the sand which is by the sea shore innumerable. These all died in faith, not having received the promises, but having seen them afar off, and were persuaded of *them,* and embraced *them,* and confessed that they were strangers and pilgrims on the earth. For they that say such things declare plainly that they seek a country. And truly, if they had been mindful of that *country* from whence they came out, they might have had opportunity to have returned. But now they desire a better *country,* that is, an heavenly: wherefore God is not ashamed to be called their God: for he hath prepared for them a city. By faith Abraham, when he was tried, offered up Isaac: and he that had received the promises offered up his only begotten *son,* Of whom it was said, That in Isaac shall thy seed be called: Accounting that God *was* able to raise *him* up, even from the dead; from whence also he received him in a figure. By faith Isaac blessed Jacob and Esau concerning things to come. By faith Jacob, when he was a dying, blessed both the sons of Joseph; and worshipped, *leaning* upon the top of his staff. By faith Joseph, when he died, made mention of the departing of the children of Israel; and gave commandment concerning his bones. By faith Moses, when he was born, was hid three months of his parents, because they saw *he was* a proper child; and they were not afraid of the king's commandment. By faith Moses, when he was come to years, refused to be called the son of Pharaoh's daughter; Choosing rather to suffer affliction with the people of God, than to enjoy the pleasures of sin for a season; Esteeming the reproach of Christ greater riches than the treasures in Egypt: for he had respect unto the recompence of the reward. By faith he forsook Egypt, not fearing the wrath of the king: for he endured, as seeing him who is invisible. Through faith he kept the passover, and the sprinkling of blood, lest he that destroyed the firstborn should touch them. By faith they passed through the Red sea as by dry *land:* which the Egyptians assaying to do were drowned. By faith the walls of Jericho fell down, after they were compassed about seven days. By faith the harlot Rahab perished not with them that believed not, when she had received the spies with peace. And what shall I more say? for the time would fail me to tell of Gedeon, and *of* Barak, and *of* Samson, and *of* Jephthae; *of* David also, and Samuel, and *of* the prophets: Who through faith subdued kingdoms, wrought righteousness, obtained promises, stopped the mouths of lions, Quenched the violence of fire, escaped the edge of the sword, out of weakness were made strong, waxed valiant in fight, turned to flight the armies of the aliens. Women received their dead raised to life again: and others were tortured, not accepting deliverance; that they might obtain a better resurrection: And others had trial of *cruel* mockings and scourgings, yea, moreover of bonds and imprisonment: They were stoned, they were sawn asunder, were tempted, were slain with the sword: they wandered about in sheepskins and goatskins; being destitute, afflicted, tormented; (Of whom the world was not worthy:) they wandered in deserts, and *in* mountains, and *in* dens and caves of the earth. And these all, having obtained a good report through faith, received not the promise: God having provided some better thing for us, that they without us should not be made perfect.

Galatians 5:22, 23 But the fruit of the Spirit is love, joy, peace, longsuffering, gentleness, goodness, faith, Meekness, temperance: against such there is no law.

Isaiah 53:1-12 Who hath believed our report? and to whom is the arm of the LORD revealed? For he shall grow up before him as a tender plant, and as a root out of a dry ground: he hath no form nor comeliness; and when we shall see him, *there is* no beauty that we should desire him. He is despised and rejected of men; a man of sorrows, and acquainted with grief: and we hid as it were *our* faces from him; he was despised, and we esteemed him not. Surely he hath borne our griefs, and carried our sorrows: yet we did esteem him stricken, smitten of God, and afflicted. But he *was* wounded for our transgressions, *he was* bruised for our iniquities: the chastisement of our peace *was* upon him; and with his stripes we are healed. All we like sheep have gone astray; we have turned every one to his own way; and the LORD hath laid on him the iniquity of us all. He was oppressed, and he was afflicted, yet he opened not his mouth: he is brought as a lamb to the slaughter, and as a sheep before her shearers is dumb, so he openeth not his mouth. He was taken from prison and from judgment: and who shall declare his generation? for he was cut off out of the land of the living: for the transgression of my people was he stricken. And he made his grave with the wicked, and with the rich in his death; because he had done no violence, neither *was any* deceit in his mouth. Yet it pleased the LORD to bruise him; he hath put *him* to grief: when thou shalt make his soul an offering for sin, he shall see *his* seed, he shall prolong *his* days, and the pleasure of the LORD shall prosper in his hand. He shall see of the travail of his soul, *and* shall be satisfied: by his knowledge shall my righteous servant justify many; for he shall bear their iniquities. Therefore will I divide him *a portion* with the great, and he shall divide the spoil with the strong; because he hath poured out his soul unto death: and he was numbered with the transgressors; and he bare the sin of many, and made intercession for the transgressors.


Revelations 3:22 He that hath an ear, let him hear what the Spirit saith unto the churches.


Isaiah 5:1-30 Now will I sing to my wellbeloved a song of my beloved touching his vineyard. My wellbeloved hath a vineyard in a very fruitful hill: And he fenced it, and gathered out the stones thereof, and planted it with the choicest vine, and built a tower in the midst of it, and also made a winepress therein: and he looked that it should bring forth grapes, and it brought forth wild grapes. And now, O inhabitants of Jerusalem, and men of Judah, judge, I pray you, betwixt me and my vineyard. What could have been done more to my vineyard, that I have not done in it? wherefore, when I looked that it should bring forth grapes, brought it forth wild grapes? And now go to; I will tell you what I will do to my vineyard: I will take away the hedge thereof, and it shall be eaten up; *and* break down the wall thereof, and it shall be trodden down: And I will lay it waste: it shall not be pruned, nor digged; but there shall come up briers and thorns: I will also command the clouds that they rain no rain upon it. For the vineyard of the LORD of hosts *is* the house of Israel, and the men of Judah his pleasant plant: and he looked for judgment, but behold oppression; for righteousness, but behold a cry. Woe unto them that join house to house, *that* lay field to field, till *there be* no place, that they may be placed alone in the midst of the earth! In mine ears *said* the LORD of hosts, Of a truth many houses shall be desolate, *even* great and fair, without inhabitant. Yea, ten acres of vineyard shall yield one bath, and the seed of an homer shall yield an ephah. Woe unto them that rise up early in the morning, *that* they may follow strong drink; that continue until night, *till* wine inflame them! And the harp, and the viol, the tabret, and pipe, and wine, are in their feasts: but they regard not the work of the LORD, neither consider the operation of his hands. Therefore my people are gone into captivity, because *they have* no knowledge: and their honourable men *are* famished, and their multitude dried up with thirst. Therefore hell hath enlarged herself, and opened her mouth without measure: and their glory, and their multitude, and their pomp, and he that rejoiceth, shall descend into it. And the mean man shall be brought down, and the mighty man shall be humbled, and the eyes of the lofty shall be humbled: But the LORD of hosts shall be exalted in judgment, and God that is holy shall be sanctified in righteousness. Then shall the lambs feed after their manner, and the waste places of the fat ones shall strangers eat. Woe unto them that draw iniquity with cords of vanity, and sin as it were with a cart rope: That say, Let him make speed, *and* hasten his work, that we may see *it:* and let the counsel of the Holy One of Israel draw nigh and come, that we may know *it!* Woe unto them that call evil good, and good evil; that put darkness for light, and light for darkness; that put bitter for sweet, and sweet for bitter! Woe unto *them that are* wise in their own eyes, and prudent in their own sight! Woe unto *them that are* mighty to drink wine, and men of strength to mingle strong drink: Which justify the wicked for reward, and take away the righteousness of the righteous from him! Therefore as the fire devoureth the stubble, and the flame consumeth the chaff, *so* their root shall be as rottenness, and their blossom shall go up as dust: because they have cast away the law of the LORD of hosts, and despised the word of the Holy One of Israel. Therefore is the anger of the LORD kindled against his people, and he hath stretched forth his hand against them, and hath smitten them: and the hills did tremble, and their carcases *were* torn in the midst of the streets. For all this his anger is not turned away, but his hand *is* stretched out still. And he will lift up an ensign to the nations from far, and will hiss unto them from the end of the earth: and, behold, they shall come with speed swiftly: None shall be weary nor stumble among them; none shall slumber nor sleep; neither shall the girdle of their loins be loosed, nor the latchet of their shoes be broken: Whose arrows *are* sharp, and all their bows bent, their horses' hoofs shall be counted like flint, and their wheels like a whirlwind: Their roaring *shall be* like a lion, they shall roar like young lions: yea, they shall roar, and lay hold of the prey, and shall carry *it* away safe, and none shall deliver *it*. And in that day they shall roar against them like the roaring of the sea: and if *one* look unto the land, behold darkness *and* sorrow, and the light is darkened in the heavens thereof.

Psalms 91:1-16 He that dwelleth in the secret place of the most High shall abide under the shadow of the Almighty. I will say of the LORD, *He is* my refuge and my fortress: my God; in him will I trust. Surely he shall deliver thee from the snare of the fowler, *and* from the noisome pestilence. He shall cover thee with his feathers, and under his wings shalt thou trust: his truth *shall be thy* shield and buckler. Thou shalt not be afraid for the terror by night; *nor* for the arrow *that* flieth by day; *Nor* for the pestilence *that* walketh in darkness; *nor* for the destruction *that* wasteth at noonday. A thousand shall fall at thy side, and ten thousand at thy right hand; *but* it shall not come nigh thee. Only with thine eyes shalt thou behold and see the reward of the wicked. Because thou hast made the LORD, *which is* my refuge, *even* the most High, thy habitation; There shall no evil befall thee, neither shall any plague come nigh thy dwelling. For he shall give his angels charge over thee, to keep thee in all thy ways. They shall bear thee up in *their* hands, lest thou dash thy foot against a stone. Thou shalt tread upon the lion and adder: the young lion and the dragon shalt thou trample under feet. Because he hath set his love upon me, therefore will I deliver him: I will set him on high, because he hath known my name. He shall call upon me, and I will answer him: I *will be* with him in trouble; I will deliver him, and honour him. With long life will I satisfy him, and shew him my salvation.

Psalms 96:1, 2 O sing unto the LORD a new song: sing unto the LORD, all the earth. Sing unto the LORD, bless his name; shew forth his salvation from day to day.

1 Peter 1:8 Whom having not seen, ye love; in whom, though now ye see *him* not, yet believing, ye rejoice with joy unspeakable and full of glory:

Psalms 22:1-31 To the chief Musician upon Aijeleth Shahar, A Psalm of David. My God, my God, why hast thou forsaken me? *why art thou so* far from helping me, *and from* the words of my roaring? O my God, I cry in the daytime, but thou hearest not; and in the night season, and am not silent. But thou *art* holy, *O thou* that inhabitest the praises of Israel. Our fathers trusted in thee: they trusted, and thou didst deliver them. They cried unto thee, and were delivered: they trusted in thee, and were not confounded. But I *am* a worm, and no man; a reproach of men, and despised of the people. All they that see me laugh me to scorn: they shoot out the lip, they shake the head, *saying,* He trusted on the LORD *that* he would deliver him: let him deliver him, seeing he delighted in him. But thou *art* he that took me out of the womb: thou didst make me hope *when I was* upon my mother's breasts. I was cast upon thee from the womb: thou *art* my God from my mother's belly. Be not far from me; for trouble *is* near; for *there is* none to help. Many bulls have compassed me: strong *bulls* of Bashan have beset me round. They gaped upon me *with* their mouths, *as* a ravening and a roaring lion. I am poured out like water, and all my bones are out of joint: my heart is like wax; it is melted in the midst of my bowels. My strength is dried up like a potsherd; and my tongue cleaveth to my jaws; and thou hast brought me into the dust of death. For dogs have compassed me: the assembly of the wicked have inclosed me: they pierced my hands and my feet. I may tell all my bones: they look *and* stare upon me. They part my garments among them, and cast lots upon my vesture. But be not thou far from me, O LORD: O my strength, haste thee to help me. Deliver my soul from the sword; my darling from the power of the dog. Save me from the lion's mouth: for thou hast heard me from the horns of the unicorns. I will declare thy name unto my brethren: in the midst of the congregation will I praise thee. Ye that fear the LORD, praise him; all ye the seed of Jacob, glorify him; and fear him, all ye the seed of Israel. For he hath not despised nor abhorred the affliction of the afflicted; neither hath he hid his face from him; but when he cried unto him, he heard. My praise *shall be* of thee in the great congregation: I will pay my vows before them that fear him. The meek shall eat and be satisfied: they shall praise the LORD that seek him: your heart shall live for ever. All the ends of the world shall remember and turn unto the LORD: and all the kindreds of the nations shall worship before thee. For the kingdom *is* the LORD'S: and he *is* the governor among the nations. All *they that be* fat upon earth shall eat and worship: all they that go down to the dust shall bow before him: and none can keep alive his own soul. A seed shall serve him; it shall be accounted to the Lord for a generation. They shall come, and shall declare his righteousness unto a people that shall be born, that he hath done *this*.

# About the Author

Bill Vincent is an Apostle and Author with Revival Waves of Glory Ministries in Litchfield, IL. Bill and his wife Tabitha work closely in every day ministry duties. Bill and Tabitha lead a team providing Apostolic over sight in all aspects of ministry, including service, personal ministry and Godly character.

Bill is a believer in Jesus Christ in the fullness of power with signs and wonders. Bill has an accurate prophetic gift, a powerful revelatory preaching anointing with miracles signs and wonders following.

Bill Vincent is no stranger to understanding the power of God, having spent over twenty years as a Minister with a strong prophetic anointing, which taught him the importance of deliverance by the power of God. Bill has more than thirty prophetic books available all over the world. Prior to starting his ministry, Revival Waves of Glory he spent the last few years as a Pastor of a Church and a traveling prophetic ministry.

Bill Vincent helps the Body of Christ to get closer to God

while overcoming the enemy. Bill offers a wide range of writings and teachings from deliverance, to the presence of God and Apostolic cutting edge Church structure. Drawing on the power of the Holy Spirit through years of experience in Revival, Spiritual Sensitivity and deliverance ministry, Bill now focuses mainly on pursuing the Presence of God and breaking the power of the devil off of people's lives.

His book Defeating the Demonic Realm was published in 2011 and has since helped many people to overcome the spirits and curses of satan. Since then Bill's books have flooded the market with his writings released just like he prophesies the Word of the Lord.

Bill Vincent is a unique man of God whom has discovered; powerful ways to pursue God's presence, releasing revelations of the demonic realm and prophetic anointing through everything he does. Bill is always moving forward at a rapid pace and there is sure to be much more released by him in upcoming years.

# Recommended Books

## By Bill Vincent

Overcoming Obstacles
Glory: Pursuing God's Presence
Defeating the Demonic Realm
Increasing Your Prophetic Gift
Increase Your Anointing
Keys to Receiving Your Miracle
The Supernatural Realm
Waves of Revival
Increase of Revelation and Restoration
The Resurrection Power of God
Discerning Your Call of God
Apostolic Breakthrough
Glory: Increasing God's Presence
Love is Waiting – Don't Let Love Pass You By
The Healing Power of God
Glory: Expanding God's Presence
Receiving Personal Prophecy
Signs and Wonders
Signs and Wonders Revelations
Children Stories
The Rapture
The Secret Place of God's Power
Building a Prototype Church
Breakthrough of Spiritual Strongholds
Glory: Revival Presence of God
Overcoming the Power of Lust
Glory: Kingdom Presence of God
Transitioning to the Prototype Church
The Stronghold of Jezebel
Healing After Divorce
A Closer Relationship With God

Cover Up and Save Yourself
Desperate for God's Presence
The War for Spiritual Battles
Spiritual Leadership
Global Warning
Millions of Churches
Destroying the Jezebel Spirit
Awakening of Miracles
Deception and Consequences Revealed
Are You a Follower of Christ
Don't Let the Enemy Steal from You!
A Godly Shaking
The Unsearchable Riches of Christ
Heaven's Court System
Satan's Open Doors
Armed for Battle
The Wrestler
Spiritual Warfare: Complete Collection
Growing In the Prophetic
The Prototype Church: Complete Edition
Faith
The Angry Fighter's Story
Understanding Heaven's Court System

## Web Site:
www.revivalwavesofgloryministries.com

www.ingramcontent.com/pod-product-compliance
Lightning Source LLC
Chambersburg PA
CBHW052056070526
44584CB00017B/2199